THE KISTE AND OGAN SOCIAL CHANGE

SERIES IN ANTHROPOLOGY

Editors

ROBERT C. KISTE   EUGENE OGAN

University of Minnesota

James M. Freeman, Professor and Chairperson of Anthropology at San José State University, is a graduate of Northwestern University, where he studied with Melville Herskovits. He received his Ph.D. in 1968 from Harvard, where he studied first with Clyde Kluckhohn and John Pelzel, and later with Cora Du Bois. Both his predoctoral and postdoctoral research were conducted in Bhubaneswar, India, under the direction of Cora Du Bois. His predoctoral study of Bhubaneswar was the first conducted by an American graduate student in that area, and his postdoctoral research was a two year follow-up study of the same community, supported by a grant from the American Institute of Indian Studies. In addition to the findings reported in the present volume, Freeman collected and translated extensive autobiographies of seven widely diverse persons who lived in Bhubaneswar. Assisted by a fellowship from the Center for Advanced Study in the Behavioral Sciences at Stanford, and by a grant awarded by the Joint Committee on South Asia of the Social Science Research Council and the American Council of Learned Societies, Freeman will devote his sabbatical year of 1976-77 to editing and integrating the autobiographies into a single narrative.

Scarcity and Opportunity in an Indian Village

JAMES M. FREEMAN

San José State University

◆◆ *Cummings Publishing Company*

Menlo Park, California • Reading, Massachusetts
London • Amsterdam • Don Mills, Ontario • Sydney

To Cora Du Bois

Cover Photo by Patricia A. Freeman.   Standing in pits of sacred water, firewalkers prepare to step onto the glowing coals. In Kapileswar village, people of all castes walk the fire as a testimony to their faith that the goddess Kali can cure them or help them out of difficulties. These popular religious rites are not disintegrating in new urban settings; on the contrary, they are increasing in importance.

Internal photos by James M. Freeman.

Library of Congress Catalog Card Number 76-4423

REVIEW COPY
NOT FOR SALE
UNTIL JAN. 2,

ISBN 0-8465-2115-6
abcdefghij-AL-79876

Cummings Publishing Company, Inc.
2727 Sand Hill Road
Menlo Park, California 94025

Contents

Illustrations

PHOTOGRAPHS

Foreword

Dr. James M. Freeman's study is the sixth volume in Cummings' series of ethnographic case studies on social and cultural change. With the possible exception of a few small populations in the most remote regions of the earth, no human group today remains unaffected by other peoples and current world events. The studies comprising this series reflect this basic state of human affairs in the latter part of the twentieth century, and they focus on a common theme: the ways in which members of contemporary societies respond to and develop strategies for coping with modifications of their social and/or physical environments. Each study is a description based on original field research by the author.

Freeman's study is concerned with the people of a relatively small village in India, a country exposed to major outside influences—alien invaders, religious movements, and British colonists—for centuries. While change has been a constant feature of their history, the lives of the villagers of Kapileswar were abruptly altered beginning in the late 1940s when a nearby community was designated as the new capital of the state of Orissa and the construction of a modern city was launched. Further change to the existing social and cultural order was precipitated by postindependence social reforms sponsored by India's national government—reforms designed to eliminate caste discrimination, expand educational and economic opportunities, and improve various public services.

Freeman's study, we believe, is significant in several ways. His analysis of his data reveals that, while some of the villagers have devised ways to reap economic rewards and improve their living standards in response to new opportunities presented by the new capital, the vast majority remain poverty-stricken, and some fight a constant battle against starvation. While acknowledging that factors of caste partly determine the responses that the villagers are making to their changed social and physical environments, Freeman differs from other scholars who argue that the caste system or Hindu religious traditions must necessarily function as impediments to change, particularly modernization. Rather, he argues convincingly that factors of caste and religion may be secondary and that economic conditions—many of which are deeply rooted in the local ecological setting—are the primary factors that entrap the disadvantaged villagers into a vicious cycle of poverty and disease.

Freeman presents an impressive array of quantitative data in support of his analysis, and he provides glances into the lives of individuals representing different segments and classes within the village. His epilogue makes some projection as to what the villagers may anticipate for their future.

This study is a contribution to the anthropology of urban life and complex societies. For students concerned with these topics, other volumes in the series, notably, David Jacobson's *Itinerant Townsmen: Friendship and Social Order in Urban Uganda* and Frank Miller's *Old Villages and a New Town: Industrialization in Mexico*, will be of interest.

University of Minnesota   ROBERT C. KISTE
Minneapolis, Minnesota   EUGENE OGAN
                                                Series Editors

Preface

When in 1962 I began the first of two field studies which led
to the writing of this book, I did not anticipate that I would be
writing about starvation among the urban poor. I went to India
with the intention of studying religious change. Specifically, I
was concerned with the effect that the construction of a new city
was having in changing the religious life-styles of Hindu temple
priests who were living in Kapileswar, an ancient temple village
that had been included in the boundaries of the new city. I assumed that the life-styles and values of the traditionally privileged
high-caste temple priests were incompatible with the new life-styles
offered by the new city, that the priests would resist the influences
of the city, and that their religion would disintegrate under the
impact of modern urbanization. I assumed, furthermore, that the
city offered new economic opportunities and benefits which the
less privileged lower castes and untouchable castes of the village
would seize, and that in doing so they would significantly alter
their life-styles.

All of my assumptions were wrong. The priests did not resist—
instead, they adapted rapidly and well to the new urban complex
at their doors, and they did so without losing their religious life-
styles. Most of the lower castes and untouchable castes failed to
benefit from the new city. The economic gap widened between
the traditionally privileged high castes and the less privileged low
and untouchable castes.

In 1970 I returned to the same urbanized temple village for
a two year follow-up study. The same trends emerged which I
had documented eight years earlier. Despite the apparent opportunities that the new city offered, the plight of those who were
at the bottom of the economic system was no better than it had

been in the previous decade, while the privileged few were benefiting immensely from the growth of the city.

There are two main facets of this study: The first is a report of how the inhabitants of an Indian temple village attempted to adapt to a new urban environment that was suddenly thrust upon them. The second is an explanation of why the growth of the city has widened the economic gap between the poor, most of whom are of low caste or untouchable caste, and the wealthy, all of whom come from middle or high castes. The book contains not only the statistical evidence on which my conclusions are based, but also lengthy statements by the villagers themselves about their own life-styles: a goldsmith relates what it is like to be out of work, out of money, and unable to find employment; an untouchable recalls being out of food, too ill to work, and starving; a wealthy landowner describes dismissing unskilled agricultural laborers when they demanded increased payments for harvesting his paddy fields.

San José, California   JAMES M. FREEMAN

Acknowledgments

My research of 1970-72 in India was funded by a Senior Research Fellowship of the American Institute of Indian Studies. I am grateful to the Institute not only for its generous support, but also for helping me to secure permission to remain in India for a second year.

I am deeply indebted to Cora Du Bois, my teacher and my friend, who first awakened my interest in problems of modernization and urbanization, and directed my first field research in India in 1962-63. To this day she has followed my work and read my writings with the dedication of a truly great teacher. I owe more than I can express to the inspiration I have gained from her encouragement and appreciation, and most of all from her penetrating criticisms of my writings.

My mother and father, Ann Freeman and Eugene Freeman, first awakened my interest in the varieties of the human experience, and thus anthropology. In the preparation of this book, they devoted countless hours to discussion of some of the topics of this book, as well as to meticulously checking the data presented in it. As academic editors themselves (managing editor and editor, respectively, of the *Monist*), my mother and father provided editorial advice and assistance which was truly indispensable.

I am especially indebted to John Pelzel for his continuing interest, encouragement, and helpful suggestions over the years regarding my field research in India, especially my collecting Indian autobiographical data, some of which appear in this book.

I am also grateful to Robert Kiste for his careful reading of this book and his detailed comments and suggestions, which I think helped me to improve the book.

I am deeply grateful to the Government of India, the Government of the state of Orissa, and the University of Utkal for graciously permitting me to remain in India and conduct research during the trying times of a war and a national emergency. I am particularly indebted to Dr. L.K. Mahapatra, Professor and Head of the Department of Anthropology, University of Utkal, for his cordial hospitality, interest in my research, and his helpful suggestions about my work. I am also grateful to Dale and Monserrat Harrison for their generous hospitality in Bhubaneswar, and for Dale's sharing with me in our numerous discussions, his knowledge of villages, nutrition, cropping patterns, and problems of economic development in Orissa.

Also deserving of my heartfelt thanks are Gagan Dash, whose excellent Oriya language instruction was invaluable, and S.M. Gani, who helped me in innumerable ways and whose sage advice was greatly appreciated.

While in India, my wife, Patricia Freeman, helped in the recording of some of the field notes, and in taking some of the more than 5000 photographs which accompany my field notes. I am grateful for her help, without which neither the notes nor the photos would have been as complete.

While this book could not have been written without the help and cooperation of many of the villagers of Kapileswar, three persons deserve special mention. Harihar Mallia, my friend and research assistant, was more than a diligent and creative field assistant. Without his contacts in the village, his endorsement of me, and his dedication to the project, my work in Kapileswar would have been virtually impossible.

In 1962, when most of the villagers of Kapileswar still feared and distrusted outsiders, Brindaban Sahoo, risking the censure of the villagers, opened up his house to me and invited me to participate in his family's activities. We have remained close friends ever since, and both my wife and I will never forget the many delightful hours we spent with the Sahoo family.

Whenever my wife and I passed by old Kia Bewa's tea stall, she rushed out and showered us with freshly fried rice cakes and informed us of the latest village gossip. Kia Bewa was not only a shopkeeper; she was also Kapileswar's most knowledgeable female ritualist, and it was from her that I acquired a deep appreciation of women's ritual life-styles. Above all, we will always cherish Kia Bewa's genuine warmth and affection for us, in the face of which our cultural differences are insignificant.

Portions of Chapter 4 and Chapter 9 first appeared in my article, "Religious Change in a Hindu Pilgrimage Center" in the *Review of Religious Research*, Vol. 16, No. 2 (Winter 1975), pp. 124-33, copyrighted by the Religious Research Association and reprinted here with their permission. Some of the data which appeared in my articles in the *Indian Anthropologist* (1971) and *Man in India* (1974b) were utilized in my newly written Chapter 5. A sharply condensed version of the untouchable's tale of starvation (Chapter 7) appeared in my recent article in the *Geographical Magazine* (in press).

JAMES M. FREEMAN

CHAPTER ONE

Introduction

Scarcity and Opportunity in Eastern India

In 1946 Bhubaneswar, an ancient Hindu temple town in eastern India, was made the capital of the state of Orissa, and in 1948 construction of the new administrative capital was begun. Bhubaneswar is famous as the site of the Lingaraj temple, built in the eleventh century A.D. The traditional religious ways of life in the older part of the city surrounding the temple had been preserved with little change for centuries. As a new rapidly expanding city was built up around the old temple community, striking and challenging rival alternatives were made available to the people of the area, and lifestyles were changed with dramatic speed and intensity. The study of these changes affords an insight into the impact of rapid urbanization on the ways of life in a traditional religious community. This book focuses in detail on the changes in life-styles which took place in one of the villages that are now suburbs of Bhubaneswar. This is the village of Kapileswar, which has its own pilgrimage temple, built 500 years ago, and thus its own pattern of a traditional religious way of life.

As a new economic and social order was being created around the very doors of the temples themselves, the inhabitants not only of the larger temple community of Bhubaneswar, but also those of the tiny villages surrounding it, found themselves swept up in a direct confrontation with a new and contrasting world. These people were confronted with new economic and social opportunities that could only be seized at the expense of abandoning their traditional occupations and activities.

An important factor in this study is the geographical setting of Bhubaneswar itself. Bhubaneswar is located in a fertile rice-growing coastal tract of eastern India. During the past century there has been considerable population growth with the result that over half the families of Kapileswar village are landless; and for the landowners, their holdings have been subdivided and fragmented through inheritance into parcels that are so small that most land-owning families ordinarily have barely enough to support them. Their plight is aggravated by natural disasters such as cyclones, droughts, floods, and epidemics, which strike on the average of six out of every ten years, producing widespread destruction of crops and property, and some loss of life.

The persons who are hit hardest by natural disasters are those at the bottom of the economic system. About 20 percent of the people of the village live on the brink of starvation. About 60 percent have a slightly higher but still marginal level of existence. Only the highest 20 percent live comfortably, without the fear of having insufficient food. The lowest 20 percent—the starving poor—lack not only food reserves, but also the cash to pay for even the cheapest of medicines. If they become ill and miss a day of work, they do not eat. Despite the growth of the new city, the starving poor have few employment opportunities and little or no chance to improve their economic condition. Although the poor are from all levels of the caste hierarchy, the lowest castes have the highest percentage of individuals who are in desperate economic straits. In some areas of India the poor have benefited significantly from modernizing influences (Randhawa 1974: 164-195). One of the aims of this book is to show why, despite apparent opportunities, the poor of Kapileswar are virtually no better off now than they were in 1962, when I began my research.

Another aim of this book is to examine the effects that scarce resources, including an unequal distribution of wealth, have in influencing directions of change. My study focuses in particular on the consequences of scarcity, not only in affecting the strategies of adaptation of different caste groups, but also its effect on the Kapileswar temple, a central institution of the village which has integrated and controlled the economic, social, political, and ritual lives of villagers in Kapileswar for the past five centuries.

In 1948, with the construction of the new city, many villagers were offered new economic opportunities which left them less completely at the mercy of an environment which had offered them alternatively abundance or disaster. As a result, the villagers, including the priests, were more responsive to the new opportunities of secular life than they might have been had the environment been more favorable.

The opportunities provided by a new city change over time. Between 1950 and 1965 Bhubaneswar experienced a period of rapid growth: new houses, roads, and public buildings were constructed; civil service positions were plentiful; and business opportunities were available for large as well as small entrepreneurs. After 1965 the growth of the city leveled off, and so did the employment opportunities available to the people of Kapileswar village. The economic fluctuations of the new city are indicated in the village statistics of changing employment, as well as in school attendance, all of which reflected processes of adaptation to changing circumstances. Thus the present study provides an excellent example of what happens to a traditional religious community and to religion itself when it is subjected to rapid urbanization and modernization, as well as economic fluctuations associated with the growth of a new city.

Sources of Data

The data are drawn from my sixteen-month field study of Kapileswar in 1962-63 and my twenty-two-month follow-up study in 1970-72. My sources of data include temple records, historical and government records of the village, my detailed census of every household of the village, observations of rituals and other activities, interviews with village leaders, ritual specialists and others with specialized information, and extensive autobiographies which I collected from Indian villagers.

The data were collected openly and with the consent of the inhabitants of Kapileswar, who understood that I was writing this book about them. Some of the villagers have read or have had translated and read to them portions of this book as well as articles that I have written about them. They have made a number of invaluable suggestions and corrections which I have heeded in writing this book. I do not, of course, expect them to agree with all of my conclusions, especially on village politics, where they are in sharp disagreement among themselves. I have tried, however, to present both sides of controversial issues with fairness.

In the past fifteen years Bhubaneswar has been the subject of intensive studies by both North American and Indian scholars. Starting in 1961 Professor Cora Du Bois of Harvard University began a ten-year study of urbanization in Bhubaneswar. She began her research with the sanction and cooperation of Dr. A. Aiyappan, who was at that time Professor and Head of the Department of Anthropology at the University of Utkal, Orissa. She continued her work later with the sanction and cooperation of his successor, Dr. L.K. Mahapatra. In addition to her own research on values, Professor Du Bois guided and inspired eleven studies of Bhubaneswar and nearby areas by Indians and North Americans, of which mine was the first by a North American. My research was conducted in an atmosphere of cordial and friendly cooperation with the Department of Anthropology, the University of Utkal, where I was a Senior Research Associate between 1970 and 1972. I am grateful to the Government of India, the Government of Orissa, and the University of Utkal for permitting me to conduct anthropological research in the village of Kapileswar, and for their unfailing courtesy during my stay.[1]

---

[1] The other studies of Bhubaneswar included those by: Jyotish Acharya 1962-65 (intermittent): The Interstitial Areas between Old and New Bhubaneswar; Harish Das, 1962-70 (intermittent): Two Urbanizing Villages; Manmohan Mahapatra, 1962-70 (intermittent): The Lingaraj Temple; Peter Grenell, 1964-65: City Planning; David Miller, 1963-65: Hindu Monastic Institutions; Alan Sable, 1965-67: Education; Susan Seymour, 1965-67: Child Rearing; Richard Shweder, 1968, 1969-70: Semantic Structures and Personality; Richard Taub, 1962-64: Government Administrators; James Preston, 1972-73: Chandi Temple of Cuttack. These studies were independent projects, but together they provide an extensive record of the changing character of Bhubaneswar. Publications from these studies include: Freeman 1971, 1974a, 1974b, 1975, 1976; Taub 1969; Grenell 1972; Sable 1976; Seymour 1975, 1976, in press; Miller and Wertz 1976.

CHAPTER TWO

The Setting

Coastal Orissa

Kapileswar and Bhubaneswar lie in the district of Puri in the 11,977-square-mile coastal tract of eastern Orissa, which is the most fertile and densely populated area of Orissa (see Map 1, page 13). The district of Puri, the central part of this tract, lies between 19°28′N and 20°35′N latitudes and between 84°29′E and 86°25′E longitudes. Bounded on the south and southeast by the Bay of Bengal, Puri District has an area of 4043 square miles. In 1971 its population was 2,339,382, which represents an increase in the density of persons per square mile from 180 persons in 1961 to 226 in 1971. Similarly, the growth rate increased from 18.39 percent between 1951 and 1961, to 25.43 percent between 1961 and 1971. The annual growth rate of Puri District of roughly 2.5 percent during the past decade is about the same as the all-Orissa and the all-India average.

The high population density of the coastal tract is a consequence of the favorable conditions it offers for paddy cultivation. The area is a level, alluvial plain intersected by several large rivers flowing from mountains in the west to the Bay of Bengal in the east. From June to September, the southwest monsoon brings the state of Orissa from 75 to 90 percent of its annual rainfall. In the coastal tract the total annual rainfall reaches 64 inches. Bhubaneswar receives 54 inches per year, with 43 inches falling during the monsoon. The degree, frequency, and timing of these rains profoundly affect cropping

patterns. Crops are as vulnerable to too much rain, with its consequent flooding, as they are to droughts. Crops are also affected
by fierce cyclonic rainstorms which originate in the Bay of Bengal.
Cyclones occur most frequently at the beginning and the end of
the monsoon season (June and October-November). These storms
often hit suddenly and with little warning to the inhabitants; and
the destruction in lives, crops, and property can be considerable.
December, January, and February are cold, dry winter months.
The coldest of these months is December which has an average
temperature of 60°F. In the summer months of March, April, and
May, coastal Orissa becomes a dessicated inferno. The soil hardens
and cracks; fitful dust storms lash the barren fields; heat-weary inhabitants pray for rain. In May the average temperature is 100°F,
but temperatures exceeding 115°F are not unknown. By early
June cultivators are anxiously looking toward the eastern sky, hoping to catch a glimpse of the black monsoon clouds on which their
survival depends (Census of India 1961:3, 11-12, 28; Sinha 1971:
14-20).

Despite periodic climatic disasters, the otherwise favorable
conditions of the coastal tract have drawn large numbers of people
to this area for many centuries, a contributing factor to its present-
day cultural makeup. Initially, Orissa was known as Kalinga and
was the seat of a powerful kingdom. The extensive remains of a
large walled city dating from that era are still visible today at the
village of Sisupalgarh, three miles from Bhubaneswar. The kingdom
of Kalinga fell to the army of the Mauryan king, Ashoka. The
great carnage from that battle with the Kalingas prompted Ashoka
to embrace Buddhism and the path of nonviolence. He commemorated his conversion by putting up a rock edict at Dhauli hill,
five miles south of the present site of Bhubaneswar. By the first
century B.C. Buddhism had been eclipsed by Jainism, largely due
to the efforts of Kharavela, one of Orissa's greatest kings. In subsequent centuries Hinduism gained ascendancy. The culmination
of this period was the construction of the 180-foot-high Lingaraj
temple in the eleventh century A.D. The Kapileswar temple, the
last of the major temples built at Bhubaneswar, was constructed in
the mid-fifteenth century by Kapilendradeva, the last powerful
Orissan king (K.C. Panigrahi 1961:175). From 1568 control of
Orissa passed into the hands of outside rulers—first Muslim Af-

Plate 1.   New Capital, Bhubaneswar.

ghans and Mughals, then Hindu Marathas from western India, and finally, in 1803, the British. During British rule there began a rapid rise in the population of the coastal section of Orissa, as well as in other parts of India. But this period was also marked by widespread economic and social disruption of Orissan society, brought about by new British land laws (Hunter 1872:267, 273-74). Although India gained its independence from the British in 1947, the effects of these changes are still evident.

The four salient characteristics of coastal Orissa just described are also very important for understanding contemporary changes in Kapileswar. First, the village is located in a fertile area particularly suitable for paddy cultivation. Second, it is highly populated, and its population density is increasing. Third, it is subject to numerous natural disasters. Finally, it is an area in which over the centuries there has been continual, although usually gradual, cultural change.

Plate 2.   Orissa State Museum, in the New Capital, Bhubaneswar.

The Expanding New Capital

Bhubaneswar, located centrally in Puri District, is bracketed by two ancient and historically important towns, Cuttack and Puri. All three towns are linked by a two-lane highway and a railway, completed in 1899, which connects coastal Orissa to cities along the eastern seaboard from Calcutta to Madras (Sahu 1956:399). In addition, daily flights between Calcutta and Bhubaneswar provide another link with the world outside Orissa. Cuttack, the preindependence capital, and the cultural and commercial center of Orissa for the past ten centuries, lies eighteen miles to the north of Bhubaneswar. It is the largest town of Orissa, with a 1971 population of 194,036. It has no place to expand, however, and apparently that is one reason why the capital was moved from Cuttack to the uninhabited rocky wastelands and scrub forests around old Bhubaneswar.

Puri, a seaside resort, pilgrim town, and district capital, with a 1971 population of 72,712, lies thirty-eight miles to the south of Bhubaneswar. Puri is perhaps the most important Hindu religious center of eastern India. It is well known for its numerous shrines and monasteries, its learned Brahmans who interpret local caste law and religious doctrine, and its numerous devotional cults, whose followers often display a high degree of religious ecstasy. The central shrine of Puri is the famous Jagannath temple, constructed at the end of the twelfth century A.D., which draws thousands of pilgrims each year (K.C. Mishra 1971; C. Panigrahi 1960: 189-92).

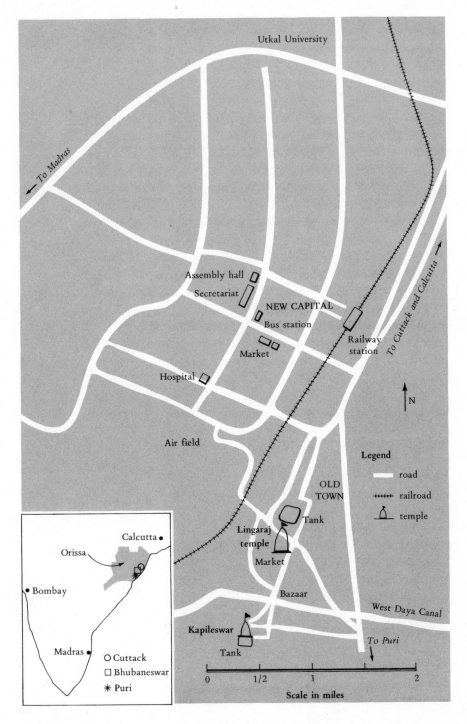

Map 1. Bhubaneswar: New Capital, Old Town, and Kapileswar, 1972.

Bhubaneswar itself stands as a symbol of contemporary India, with its New Capital buildings perched atop a hill and its Old Town below. The New Capital was constructed two and one-half miles from the old pilgrim center; as forests were cleared and buildings erected, government officers were transferred from Cuttack to the New Capital. Each working day several thousand government servants, clad in the uniforms of their office rank (spotless white for clerks and rough khaki for messengers) cycle or trudge up wide avenues past government-built housing to government offices. Many of them work in the imposing state secretariat building, three stories high and one-quarter of a mile long.

The population of Bhubaneswar has grown rapidly, from 16,512 persons in 1951, to 38,211 in 1961, to 105,514 in 1971 (Census of India 1971:46). The growth rate of 131.4 percent between 1951 and 1961 was the highest of any Orissan town, while the growth rate of 176.1 percent between 1961 and 1971 was the second highest among Orissa's twenty-five largest towns.

Part of the reason for this rapid growth is that the boundaries of the town have been extended to include twenty-one villages, including the village of Kapileswar. These villages, as well as the town, are governed by administrative officials who, until the late 1960s, were appointed by the state of Orissa rather than elected to their posts.[1]

Despite twenty years of growth, the character of the new section of town has not altered appreciably. The New Capital remains a planned community of strangers, an administrative town of elected officials and government workers. There is little or no industry. While markets and shopping centers have sprung up to cater to the needs of government workers, the commercial importance of the town lags far behind Cuttack. However, the construction of numerous colleges and universities at Bhubaneswar signifies the start of the New Capital as a cultural center.

The effects of the New Capital on the surrounding villages have been far reaching. Due to housing shortages in Bhubaneswar, strangers rented houses in nearby villages. Siripur, a community

---

[1] The council of state-appointed officials which administers Bhubaneswar is called a Notified Area Council (N.A.C.). For clarity I shall refer to the N.A.C. officials as municipal administrators.

Plate 3.   A business section along Cuttack-Puri Road in the New Capital, Bhubaneswar.

composed originally of Hinduized tribal Saoras, was engulfed by the city. And in Kapileswar, strangers moved into caste-segregated neighborhoods which had never before housed strangers of another caste. As the open spaces between the New Capital and the Old Town rapidly filled with new housing, land became scarce, and rents and land prices soared. City officials installed new public facilities throughout the municipality. Kapileswar, on the far side of the Old Town, received electric lights, water spigots, drains, and improved roads. There were substantial improvements in public health, but these public benefits were not distributed uniformly. Some facilities were brought into the high-caste wards of Kapileswar as early as 1961. In contrast, as late as 1971, three of the five wards of an untouchable field laborer caste, called Bauri, still had received no new public facilities whatsoever. Just before the national and local elections of 1971 an electric line was strung through one of these Bauri wards, but no public lights were installed, and no other facilities have been added since then.

The Old Town

It takes only a few minutes to travel by bus from the planned buildings and wide avenues of the New Capital to the crowded houses and narrow lanes of Old Town Bhubaneswar. At the entrance to the Old Town, with the massive grey tower of the Lingaraj temple looming in the distance, there is an enormous 1300-by-700-foot pond with stone steps, the Bindusagar tank, fed by an underground stream, where pilgrims and other devotees of Lingaraj bathe before entering the temple. Lining the winding road which leads to the tank are centuries-old, ruined temples, half-buried in the reddish dirt, surrounded by newly built pink and blue stone

Plate 4.   A small shop-stall, Old Town Bhubaneswar. The shop sells such articles as dry snacks, cigarettes, toothpaste, dolls, syrup concentrate, perfumed bath soaps, and laundry powder.

houses, as well as by rickety wooden betel and cigarette stalls, tea shops, food stalls, medicine shops, and two multistoried brick and lime-plastered rest houses, which all cater to the pilgrim trade, the main occupation of the Old Town.

Moving beyond the tank along the road that leads to Kapileswar, the traveler passes the stone lions guarding the gate and the Lingaraj temple, with its adjacent, biweekly market, which is located on the site of the old palace grounds of the Kesari Dynasty kings. On Mondays and Thursdays the market fills with jostling crowds of prospective buyers and curiosity seekers. As is the custom, most of the market-goers are men. While friends meet and gossip, shoppers pick through mounds of potatoes, ginger, hot green peppers, and plantains, or inspect the quality of rice or lentils. Spirited bargaining begins, sometimes interrupted by an anguished vendor's curse as a roaming cow deftly snatches one of his eggplants.

Beyond the market there are tea shops, offices, residences, and the cramped shops of goldsmiths, tailors, and cloth merchants, hazy with incense. About one-half mile south of the Lingaraj temple, the road widens into a newly built bazaar area containing some ten wooden stalls and small stone shops. Most of these are owned and run by the villagers of Kapileswar. The businesses include food shops, a laundry, a rice mill, a bicycle repair shop, a bicycle parts shop, and a picture-framing stall. All of them except the rice mill were established in 1966 or after. Twenty years ago, the bazaar area was a forest separating Kapileswar from the Old Town. Today it marks the extension of the city to the village.

The Physical Environment around Kapileswar

The new bazaar area lies just north of the village of Kapileswar (see Map 2, page 24). Northwest of the village is a barren, rocky field, pitted with the terraced excavations of stone quarries. These stones are used for building houses in the Bhubaneswar area. Only a few trees at the edge of the village stand as reminders of the forest of twenty years earlier. The northern edge of Kapileswar is bisected by the West Daya Canal, a large government-built project which was started in 1963 and was as yet unfinished and unusable

in 1972. A small river, the Gangua, passes within one-fourth mile
of Kapileswar's southeast boundary, and provides the main source
of water for the winter rice crop, which is grown in paddy fields
to the south, southeast, and west of the village.

Winter rice (planted in June and harvested between November
and January) is almost the sole crop grown by the villagers, although some of them also grow pulses, sugar cane, and a few vegetables. Several individuals have fruit trees—mostly guava, mango,
and jackfruit—which are not cared for systematically. Despite
the presence of the Gangua River, the villagers complain of difficulties in regulating water for their crops. In fact, they depend
heavily on the unpredictable monsoon, over which they have no
control. The degree and timing of the monsoon affect the growth
of paddy crops not once, but many times during the course of
cultivation. At any one of these crucial periods, irregularities in
the monsoon may destroy the crop. If there is no rain at the end
of the hot, dry, summer months (March through May) to soften
the parched and hardened soil, cultivators cannot plow the land

Plate 5.   An untouchable Bauri sharecropper plows his master's
fields.

with their iron-tipped, bullock-drawn wooden plows, nor flatten
and weed the land, nor can they sow seeds. But if the rain is excessive at this time, it becomes too muddy to plow, and seedlings
may be washed away, or young plants may be submerged for long
periods of time and thus be destroyed. Plowing must be done
three to four times, but each time it can be done only immediately
after the proper amount of rainfall has made a particular field
workable. In Kapileswar, the higher lands, which depend solely on
rainfall, may not be ready for plowing until long after the lower
lands, which can be irrigated with river water. In either case, there
is a time beyond which it becomes too late to sow seeds and expect to get a crop. If a cultivator finds himself in this position,
the only thing he can do is to wait until the transplanting stage,
and then, at considerable expense, buy plants from another cultivator.

Some of the difficulties faced by the farmers of Kapileswar
could have been avoided. For example, for many years the village
maintained a stone dam across the Gangua River. In 1955 a great
flood washed away the river banks making the dam an island in
the middle of the widened river. The villagers never repaired this
dam, and thus did not provide themselves with a supply of water
to tide themselves over during times of drought. This was because
only a few individuals in Kapileswar depended entirely on cultivation. The majority of the villagers had additional sources of income,
either from the New Capital or from the village. Moreover, they
did not concern themselves about potential problems of drought
until they became immediately affected by it. Finally, to rebuild
the dam would have required a massive cooperative effort involving several hundred villagers. There was no leader in Kapileswar
at that time who could organize such a project.

In the past, flooding from the river brought mud from the
hills. This benefited paddy cultivation, provided that the flooding
was not excessive. With present government flood control measures, flooding from the Gangua now is rare; cultivators make up
for the loss of silt by spreading manure and charcoal on the fields.
However, there has developed a new source of flooding that is not
beneficial. Rainwater from the New Capital drains into the low-
lying fields of Kapileswar and washes away the top soil. In order
to counteract this, some cultivators throw manure on their fields
during the middle of the rainy season.

Another recurrent monsoon problem for the cultivators of Kapileswar centers around transplanting paddy. Transplanting distributes the crop evenly over different lands. Though many fields which depend solely on the monsoon have insufficient water and thus are not suitable for the early stages of paddy cultivation, they may be suitable for transplanted paddy later in the season. The problem is that there is more of this transplant-receiving land than there is transplant-giving land. Moreover, many landholdings are fragmented, making it difficult to transplant from one plot to a distant plot.

Even after transplanting, excessive or insufficient rain can still damage crops. One of the most feared disasters, cyclonic storms, occurs frequently in late October, just before harvest, when high winds accompanied by heavy rains devastate the flowering paddy plants.

Natural Disasters in Puri District and in Kapileswar

Natural disasters, particularly those associated with the monsoon, appear to be the rule rather than the exception both for Puri District and for Kapileswar. The Census of India, 1961, provides a revealing summary of major natural disasters which have befallen Puri District and of their grim consequences, from the great Bengal Famine of 1770 to the extensive floods of 1955, 1958, and 1960. During the sixty-year period between 1901 and 1960 there were only twenty-five average-to-good years in which there were sufficient crops and the absence of epidemics. In the remaining thirty-five years one or more calamities caused considerable loss of life and widespread destruction of crops and property. There were fourteen years of excessive rain or flooding, eleven of droughts, four of big October-November cyclones, six of unspecified weather conditions which ruined the paddy crop, along with sixteen years in which virulent epidemics of smallpox, malaria, influenza, cholera or dysentery, or a combination of these diseases decimated the population (Census of India 1961:11-12, 28).

Within the eighteen-year period from 1955 to 1972, the village of Kapileswar had only four good paddy harvests, but fourteen

years of natural calamities, including eleven years of excessive
rain or flooding, three fires, six damaging cyclones, eight years
of drought or insufficient rainfall, six years in which there were
epidemics of debilitating diseases, and one year in which insects
totally destroyed the pulse crop. A community such as Kapileswar
usually can withstand a year of calamities but becomes extremely
hard-pressed when several successive years of disasters occur. For
example, the four-year period between 1969 and 1972 was one of
recurrent disasters, starting in 1969 with an August cyclone followed immediately by thirteen days of heavy, continuous rain.
The result was massive destruction of mud and thatch buildings
and of lowland crops; loss of livestock, man-hours of work, and
income; and widespread hunger among those who depended on a
daily wage for their food and who had no food stored at home.
Also, plants for transplanting were not available around Bhubaneswar, so Kapileswar cultivators had to buy them from market villages fifteen to twenty miles away. The cost was so prohibitive
that many cultivators abandoned growing lowland crops that year.
In September, with insufficient rainfall and insufficient water in
the Gangua River, the higher lands dried out; and cultivators tried
unsuccessfully to irrigate them with water from their lower lands.
Aided by government funds, the villagers in desperation started to
construct a temporary mud dam across the Gangua. A nearby
downstream village, facing a similar water shortage, requested the
villagers of Kapileswar to delay completing the dam for a week.
Since the people of Kapileswar refused, the inhabitants of the
other village broke the dam one night, which led to three days
of violent clashes between the rival villagers before the water dispute was settled. The year 1969 ended with a 40 percent loss of
paddy and a 60 percent loss of pulses.

In the following year, 1970, a drought in June just after sowing required that the seeds be removed from the ground and re-
planted. From July to August the excessive rains and flooding
destroyed the crops, and most cultivators were unable to transplant
again. A very few people did start all over again; although their
crops matured late, they got a good harvest. The others got little
or nothing. The overall loss of paddy was 60 percent.

The third year of this exemplary disaster period, 1971, began
with insufficient rain during the months of January to March, with

a consequent total loss of the pulse crop. In July fifteen days of flooding from water draining from the New Capital destroyed much of the paddy crop, requiring many cultivators to buy new plants from other villagers. In September excessive flooding from the river inhibited the growth of the crop; a month later the crop was adversely affected by insufficient water, and at the end of October a great cyclone destroyed the flowering plants. Fifty percent of the crop was lost in Kapileswar. In some of the harder-hit areas of coastal Orissa the loss was total (Government of Orissa 1972).

Finally, 1972 was characterized by a severe drought through the summer months and well into June, which delayed plowing and sowing. In early June a cyclone and fire damaged village houses and completely destroyed three hundred houses in the Old Town, including numerous shops owned by Kapileswar villagers.

Plate 6.   The effects of a cyclone and fire occurring on June 6, 1972.

There was flooding in July, followed by a massive outbreak of typhoid in the village. Cultivators were pessimistic about the expected outturn of paddy when I left the village in July. The price of rice in the market had already nearly doubled in six months, a somber indication of scarcity brought about by the destruction of the previous year's harvest by the cyclone.[2]

The Wards of the Village

Kapileswar is a nucleated village, that is, the houses are crowded together within a well-defined boundary, with the fields of the village surrounding it.[3] (See Map 2, page 24.)

The road into Kapileswar leads into one of the high-caste streets of the village. Situated at the village entrance there is a small stone temple; across the street from it stands a two-story stone residence with intricately carved railings and windows. Beyond these buildings the treeless street is lined with closely clustered red mud huts and occasional stone dwellings under grey thatch roofs or, infrequently, corrugated iron roofs. Open stone drains run past an open well. There are no empty spaces or house plots.

At the far end of the street there stands a small, windowless hut which is the neighborhood clubhouse. It contains palm leaf manuscripts on astrology, magic, healing, and religion.

---

[2] The villagers have written me that 1973 brought them no relief from catastrophes: about two hundred villagers became victims of cholera, and 1974 was characterized by a severe drought.

[3] There are two other main settlement patterns of Indian villages—hamleted and dispersed. Cohn describes a hamleted village as one in which "there is usually a central settlement, several hamlets, and satellite settlements scattered over the fields of the village" (Cohn 1971:142). In a dispersed village pattern, "there is no obvious village, because homesteads are dispersed, generally on or near the fields owned or worked on by the agriculturalists" (Cohn 1971:132-43). The three settlement patterns are found in different ecological settings in India and are associated with different cropping patterns (see Cohn 1971:143).

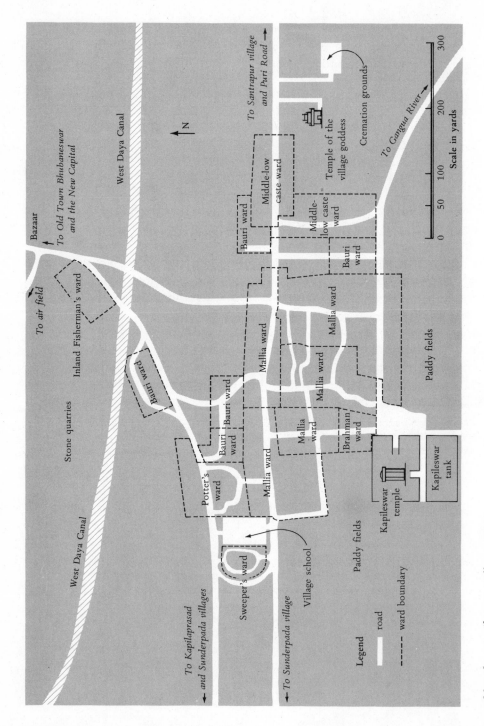

Map 2. Kapileswar Village, 1972.

Plate 7.   A Mallia ward of Kapileswar. A dead calf, considered ritually de-filing, is left for the untouchable Sweeper to drag away. The stone house (right) belongs to a wealthy businessman.

All of the sixteen caste-segregated wards of the village are crowded, and most have clubhouses and small shrines. The higher-caste villagers live in six wards in the central and oldest portion of the village. The streets of the wards converge on the square in front of the Kapileswar temple in the southwest corner of the village. Adjacent to the temple there is a large tank (pond with stone steps), where the villagers bathe and wash their clothes. The tank is stocked with fish. Both the tank and its fish are owned by a caste of temple servants, called Mallia, who occupy five of the central wards. The sixth is inhabited by a caste of Brahman cooks. Almost all of the people who have hereditary jobs in the temple live in these six high-caste wards.

Most of the wealth of the village is concentrated in these six
neighborhoods, as is rather obviously indicated by the numerous
new stone houses, and houses with stone, corrugated iron, or tile
roofs—an important protection against fire. These streets also
contain most of the seventeen food stores, tea shops, and small
businesses of the village. All but three of these were established
since 1950. The high-caste streets also have most of the public
facilities of the village, including five of the village's six paved
roads, seven of the nine public electric lights, eleven of the twenty-
two village wells, and five of the ten street spigots. Unquestionably,
the high castes and the wealthy garner greater benefits from the
municipality than do the poorer, lower-caste people who live in
peripheral pockets of the village.

Caste segregation is carried beyond isolated location. Paths
connect the high-caste wards, but in most instances there is no way
to go directly from one low-caste ward to another. Thus in the
northwest corner of the village, untouchable Sweepers, the village
Potters, and the caste of untouchable Bauris live adjacent to each
other yet are physically separated to such an extent that daily
activities and even festivals take place in one ward and go completely unnoticed by the inhabitants of the other two wards.

With such emphasis on residential segregation by caste, it is
no accident that eight of the ten lower-caste wards are single-
caste neighborhoods. The exceptions are two multicaste wards
at the eastern edge of the village inhabited by craftsmen, tradesmen,
and cultivators of middle-caste rank. A few Brahmans who recently
moved to Kapileswar also live there. These two wards together have
three public wells, an open drain, a pipe water outlet, and a public
electric light. At the lowest extreme, three of the five Bauri wards
have virtually no public facilities. None of the Bauri wards have
paved streets or drains; only one has a public light, and only two
have water spigots. There are no stone houses among these landless field laborers, only mud and thatch dwellings which are the
first to be destroyed during times of fire, cyclone, or flood.

CHAPTER THREE

The Castes
of Kapileswar

The Organization of Castes in Kapileswar

Kapileswar is populated solely by Hindus stratified into twenty castes.[1] The term "caste" here refers not to the all-India classification, called *varna*, but to local endogamous groups which the inhabitants of Orissa, like other North Indians, call *jati*. These castes are said to be ranked on the basis of ritual cleanliness. The lowest castes of the village are allegedly born ritually unclean, and therefore are potential polluters of high-caste people. Ordinarily, high-caste people do not eat or drink with those whom they consider lower since they believe that cooked food and water transfer pollution. Most of the lower castes engage in menial, low-paying hereditary occupations associated with low status or ritual uncleanliness, which range from plowing, which is lowly regarded because it entails killing organisms in the soil, to scavenging and carrying night-soil from the houses of high-caste villagers. The hereditary occupations of the highest castes, on the other hand, focus primarily on

---

[1] Indian villages vary in size, caste composition, and political structure. Cohn follows Beals' classification in summarizing these types. Some small villages consist of a single caste that is governed by a single caste council. Other small villages have several castes that are governed by a single headman. Kapileswar is characteristic of a third type of organization, a multicaste village with a dominant caste that controls the village (Beals 1961:27-34 cited in Cohn 1971:143-47). A dominant caste is defined on pages 32-33.

religion and so are believed to involve less risk of pollution. The caste rules of marriage, commensality, and occupation are largely but not entirely followed in Kapileswar.

In recent years it has become clear that many earlier preconceptions about the caste system were misleading because they focused almost exclusively on the ideal system. In theory an individual's caste is determined by birth and is part of a rigid and unchanging hierarchy with clear-cut rankings. In practice there is considerable caste mobility and change. Ordinarily this is group, not individual, mobility. It usually takes several generations for a caste to raise its status. Caste mobility is not a new development but a process which has been going on for centuries (Srinivas 1966:1-45; Barber 1968:18-35). Contrary to theory, villagers often vigorously disagree about caste rankings (Berreman 1965:115-29).[2] Although the villagers of Kapileswar dispute these rankings, the castes of Kapileswar can be arranged in a hierarchy of caste blocks which provide a rough indication of caste ranking, as shown in Table 3.1. Villagers dispute rankings within these blocks but not between them. The blocks correspond generally to the hierarchy of hereditary privileges and ritual services of castes in the Kapileswar temple.[3]

---

[2] Furthermore, scholars are not in agreement concerning the appropriate criteria to use in assigning caste rankings (see Berreman 1965:115-20; Mahar, P. 1959:115-26; Marriott 1960, 1968:133-71).

[3] In Table 3.1 and throughout the book I use the term "household" to mean, following Shah's definition, "a residential and domestic unit composed of one or more persons living under the same roof and eating food cooked in a single kitchen" (Shah 1974:8). Almost all of the 594 households of the village are comprised of exclusive kinship units. The three exceptions are wealthy households in which a personal servant also resides. For the purposes of this study, the servants are listed separately from the households in which they work. The term "family" refers to a "kinship unit whose members may be living in more than one household" (Shah 1974:108). The Brahman caste names of Khuntia, Misra, Nanda, and Dash, and the caste names of Mallia and Bauri, which have no English translation, are italicized in the tables but not in the text, where these names are used frequently.

Table 3.1 The Caste Distribution of Households in Kapileswar in 1972

Caste Names		Households No.	%	Individuals No.	%
Native Residents					
High					
Khuntia (Brahman)		13	2.2	76	2.7
Misra (Brahman)		11	1.9	56	2.0
Other Brahman		3	.5	12	.4
Mallia		225	37.8	1063	37.3
Middle					
Khandait	'Militia'	11	1.9	66	2.3
Guria	'Confectioner'	10	1.7	80	2.8
Sunar Bania	'Goldsmith'	11	1.9	52	1.8
Potoli Bania	'Betel Seller'	3	.5	34	1.2
Teli	'Oilpresser'	17	2.9	99	3.5
Chasa	'Cultivator'	18	3.0	101	3.5
Gauda	'Herdsman'	9	1.5	46	1.6
Kamar	'Blacksmith'	1	.2	5	.2
Badhei	'Carpenter'	2	.3	8	.3
Low					
Kumbhar	'Potter'	25	4.2	95	3.3
Keuta	'Inland Fisherman'	21	3.5	111	3.7
Barik	'Barber'	3	.5	14	.5
Untouchable					
Dhoba	'Washerman'	4	.7	15	.5
Bauri		100	16.8	456	15.9
Hadi	'Sweeper'	11	1.9	80	2.8
Totals: Native		(498)	(83.9)	(2469)	(86.3)
Strangers					
High					
Brahman (many surnames)		28	4.7	95	3.3
Karan	'Scribe'	8	1.3	36	1.3
Middle					
Guria	'Confectioner'	5	.8	24	.8
Sunar Bania	'Goldsmith'	3	.5	15	.5
Teli	'Oilpresser'	4	.7	22	.8
Other business castes		6	1.0	26	.9
Gauda	'Herdsman'	1	.2	3	.1
Chasa	'Cultivator'	5	.8	15	.5
Khandait	'Militia'	5	.8	15	.5
Badhei	'Carpenter'	1	.2	5	.2
Low					
Kumbhar	'Potter'	2	.3	17	.6
Keuta	'Inland Fisherman'	4	.7	13	.5
Nolia	'Sea Fisherman'	22	3.7	109	3.8
Untouchable					
Hadi	'Sweeper'	2	.3	5	.2
Totals: Strangers		(96)	(16.0)	(400)	(14.0)
Totals: Village		594	99.9	2869	100.3

Native Residents

The distribution of wealth, political power, and ritual privileges in Kapileswar depends upon the position a caste holds in the Kapileswar temple. The two highest and most important castes of the temple are the Brahmans and the Mallias. They own most of the land and wealth of Kapileswar. In addition, they are numerically predominant, comprising 42.4 percent of the population of the village.

The villagers of Kapileswar frequently refer to the Brahmans by their surnames such as Misra, Khuntia, Nanda, and Dash. This custom is not usually extended to other castes whose surnames and caste names differ. The two most frequently occurring Brahman names in Kapileswar are Misra and Khuntia. There are eleven Misra households consisting of fifty-six individuals, or 2 percent of the population of Kapileswar. The Misras are considered the highest Brahmans in the village. Accordingly, they perform the highest temple function, supplying sacred incantations to Mallia temple servants. Some Misras also work as astrologers. There are thirteen Khuntia households consisting of seventy-six persons or 2.7 percent of the village population. They are generally considered the lowest Brahmans of the village, and their performance as the temple's hereditary cooks is considered a ritually lower task than that of the Misras. There is no intermarriage between the Khuntias and the Misras, and in most matters they act as independent groups. Consequently, it is useful to follow the custom of the villagers by referring to the Brahmans by their surnames. The remaining three households of Brahmans (twelve individuals) do not have hereditary services at the Kapileswar temple. Many of these Brahmans work as family priests who perform marriage, funeral, and other life-cycle and purification ceremonies for the higher-caste families of the village.

The Mallia caste, found only in Kapileswar, is the largest caste of the village, with 1063 individuals, or 37 percent of the village population. The hereditary occupation of the Mallias is service to the deity of the Kapileswar temple. They are what Srinivas calls a "dominant caste," that is, a landowning caste controlling a local area or village on the basis of its numerical strength and economic power and also commanding a high place in the

Plate 8.   Morning prayers at the *tulasi* 'sweet basil' plant which is sacred to the god Vishnu.

local hierarchy (Srinivas 1966:10). The Mallias base their power on their inherited position as managers of the Shiva temple of Kapileswar, their control of most of the temple lands, their overwhelming numerical strength, and their custom of village endogamy. This is an unusual custom in coastal Orissa, and it gives the Mallias greater cohesion than other village castes whose relatives are thinly spread in an intervillage network.

One of the distinctive characteristics of both Mallias and Brahmans is their great emphasis on ritual purification. Almost all of their numerous rituals focus on eliminating pollution. Early morning bathing and prayer at several shrines, a process which for men can take hours, is an essential element of the life-style of these castes. Women have the important responsibility of keeping the kitchens ritually pure. It is not possible for an individual or a family to remain pure indefinitely, as there are constant risks of becoming polluted by contact with lower castes or by changes within the family. For example, the death of an individual marks his entire family as polluted and therefore "untouchable" as far as the rest of their caste is concerned. Caste members will not accept food from them or enter their house. They are considered polluted for ten days, after which a funeral ceremony is performed which purifies them and reinstates them in their caste. The death of a cow, a sacred, highly revered animal in India, also can lead to the pollution of an individual. During the cyclone of October 1971, a Mallia woman tied a cow in its stall. The wall of the cowshed collapsed, killing the cow. After consulting an ancient palm leaf manuscript on religious law, a Brahman of the village decreed that the Mallia woman was responsible for the death of the cow. Her polluting *papa* 'sin' could be removed only if she performed the *gobadhia* 'cow-death expiation ceremony', which included drinking *panchagavia* 'the five holy substances of the

Plate 9.   The *gobadhia* 'cow-death expiation ceremony'. In order to purify herself, a Mallia woman sips the *panchagavia* 'five holy substances of the cow'. Her family's Barber waits to pour more of the mixture into her right palm.

Plate 10.   A Brahman sacred thread ceremony—a high-caste boys' rite of
initiation that emphasizes ritual purity. Completion of the ceremony en-
titles the initiate to perform the rituals of Brahmans.

cow'—milk, curds, clarified butter, urine, and dung. The five holy
substances of the cow are used whenever it is believed that an individual has become greatly polluted. Other castes also are concerned with rituals of purification but ordinarily not to the degree
and intensity of the Brahmans and Mallias.

There are three important castes of middle rank in Kapileswar.
The Confectioners, who live in the street of the Brahmans, are
highly regarded because of their hereditary service of presenting
sweets to the temple deity. The most important business caste of
the village is the Oilpresser caste, a relatively wealthy caste of landowners, moneylenders, and shopkeepers. (None of the Kapileswar

Oilpressers engage in their hereditary occupation.)[4]

The third important middle caste of Kapileswar is the Cultivator caste. Although many Cultivators are landless sharecroppers, they are by far the best farmers of the village and the most innovative and receptive to new farming techniques. The Cultivators, the only caste of Kapileswar which has attempted cooperative farming, are ranked lower in Kapileswar than in many other Orissan villages. This is because the powerful Mallias, their landlords, wish to maintain social distance from them; however, on rare occasions Mallias marry Cultivator women, provided that they are not from Kapileswar. These are usually second marriages of poor Mallia widowers.

Among the low castes, all of which are considered "clean" (in contrast to "untouchable"), there are two castes entrusted with important ritual functions in the village. The Potters are the sole suppliers of pots for sacred food cooked in both the village temple and in the Lingaraj temple of Old Town Bhubaneswar. This is a never-ending task since, according to custom, pots for sacred food may be used only once and then must be destroyed. The Potters of Kapileswar are active participants in a Potter caste council, encompassing fifteen villages, which regulates the conduct of its caste members and settles disputes. Potter leaders of each village make up the intervillage council.

The other low caste with important ritual functions is the Barber caste. The Barbers are the hereditary custodians of the shrine of the village goddess—a shrine second in importance only to the Kapileswar temple. Although a low caste, the Barbers—both men and women—have an important role in every life-cycle ritual conducted by the middle and high castes of the village.

There are three castes in Kapileswar whom the high-caste villagers consider "untouchable." The Sweeper caste is the lowest of the three. Because of the alleged potential of the Sweepers for transmitting pollution, they are forced to live in a segregated ham-

---

[4] Throughout the state of Orissa, Oilpressers participate in an extensive intervillage caste association which has the potential for becoming a politically important power group (Pattnaik and Ray 1960:9-80). The Oilpressers of Kapileswar have not been particularly active in this group.

Plate 11.   An untouchable Sweeper makes a cow-hide drum.

let at the western edge of the village. Refused the use of public wells, as well as admittance to schools, shops, and village shrines, including the Kapileswar temple, the Sweepers are not welcome on higher-caste streets, except when they come to carry away nightsoil or the carcasses of dead cows. They eat the meat of these animals and use the hides to make drums. As the musicians of the village, they are expected to perform at public ceremonies of the village as well as for the private rituals of high-caste families. One of the most distinctive characteristics of the Sweepers is their dialect, which is not easily understood by other castes of the village.[5]

---

[5] A published example of Sweepers' dialect is found in Gopinath Mohanty's Oriya language novel, *Harijan* 1967.

The Bauris, the second largest caste of the village, with 456 individuals in 100 households, are considered slightly higher in rank than the Sweepers. The Bauris also live in segregated hamlets of the village and are subject to roughly the same forms of discrimination as the Sweepers. The only exception is that the Bauris are allowed to enter the outer compound of the Kapileswar temple. Economically, these landless laborers are even worse off than the impoverished Sweepers. Their primary occupation is agricultural day labor for the landed and wealthy high castes of the village.

The life and outlook of the Bauris, vastly different from those of their high-caste employers, are based primarily on uncertainty of employment and food and on fear of reprisal for disobeying the dictates of the higher castes. Unlike the higher castes, their approach to religion is primarily pragmatic; that is, they turn to deities for help during times of crisis and otherwise pay little attention to religious rituals or prayer. Some of their neighborhood shrines remain unattended and unused for months at a time. In addition, family life among the Bauris departs greatly from high-caste Hindu ideals and practices. Among the high castes of Kapileswar not a single widow has been allowed to remarry. Divorce is strongly disapproved of and infrequent; only in extremely rare circumstances have high-caste divorced women without children been allowed to remarry. In contrast, among the Bauris widow remarriage is the rule, not the exception; and divorce and remarriage similarly are quite widespread for Bauri women. The brittleness of Bauri families is a consequence of the economic and social independence of the women, almost all of whom are full-time earners. If a Bauri woman does not like the way she is being treated, either by her husband or his family, she simply leaves for her father's house; and the husband and his family are deprived of a substantial income.

Another distinctive characteristic of the Bauris is their extensive intervillage caste network, involving both hereditary ritual and secular leaders and including several hundred villages in Orissa. The ultimate authority for Bauri caste regulations rests with the head of a monastery in the sacred pilgrim town of Puri. The monastery was founded in the sixteenth century by the Bengali religious leader Chaitanya, whose *bhakti* 'devotional' worship transcended the narrow boundaries of caste. Over time, however, the monastery became associated with the Bauris. In 1972 and 1973 some young, educated

Bauris tried unsuccessfully to use this ancient intervillage organization as a vehicle for mobilizing the Bauris of Orissa to break away from economic and political exploitation by higher castes.[6]

The Washerman caste is the highest ranking of the untouchables of Kapileswar. Unlike the other untouchable castes, the four households of Washermen live in high-caste and middle-caste wards. In other respects, however, they are treated like the Bauris.

The Sweepers, Bauris, and Washermen are exploited castes at the bottom of the economic and social scale. Contemporary Indian laws prohibit discrimination against groups such as these, who formerly were called "untouchables." Nevertheless, throughout India the success of ex-untouchables in improving their economic and social position has, not surprisingly, been quite uneven and sparse (Mahar, M. 1972; Cohn 1955:53-77).

Strangers in Kapileswar

One of the most significant developments over the past two decades has been the steady increase of strangers residing in Kapileswar. In 1962 two hundred twenty-nine strangers lived in Kapileswar, and they comprised 9.7 percent of the population of the village. One hundred thirty-two of them (57.6 percent) came from high castes which stress education and government service jobs. Many of the strangers who worked as government servants said that they would remain in Kapileswar only until they could find a better house in the New Capital. They considered the villagers illiterate and uncouth, and they pointedly remained aloof from village affairs. However, a few high-caste strangers bought land, built stone houses in the village, and entered actively into village life. All of these strangers were native inhabitants of Orissa.

By 1972 newcomers to Kapileswar had increased to 400 individuals, and comprised 14 percent of the total population of the village. Six strangers came from states outside of Orissa, including Bengal, Andhra, and Tamil Nadu. While many of the new strangers were Brahman civil servants, the most spectacular increase occurred

---

[6] Such movements are frequently found in India (see Rudolph and Rudolph 1967:36-64).

among the Sea Fishermen, a low caste which is not native to Kapileswar. With regard to their numerical strength, in 1962 the Sea
Fishermen ranked eighteenth out of twenty castes with a population of ten persons. By 1972 they ranked fourth in the population
of the village with 109 individuals. They sell dried fish to the bur-
geoning population of the New Capital.

There has been a rapid turnover of strangers in Kapileswar.
Forty-five percent (27 out of 60) of the households of strangers
that were recorded in my 1962 census of Kapileswar were no
longer in the village by 1972. Of the 96 households of strangers
in Kapileswar in 1972, only nine had been in the village prior to
1950; 24 of them arrived between 1950 and 1962; and the remaining 63 came between 1962 and 1972. In 1972 seventy-five
percent (69 out of 96) of the households of strangers were in
Mallia wards or in the Potter ward, where new houses were built
for renting. As in the previous decade, most of the high-caste
civil servants hoped to move into better housing in the New Capital.
The Sea Fishermen, in contrast, say that they prefer to remain in
Kapileswar, where the rents are lower than in the New Capital and
where they save even more by crowding ten and twenty individuals
into a room.

In summary, the influx of both Brahmans and Sea Fishermen
reveals not only clear-cut occupational selectivity by caste among
strangers in Kapileswar, but also indicates that there is a range of
opportunities, from civil service to selling in the market, that draws
migrants to the New Capital and its surrounding villages.

Jajmani 'Ritual Service' Relationships

The Mallias are the central caste in an intercaste system of
hereditary ritual services known as the *jajmani* system. This system
appears to be widespread although not universal throughout India.
Kolenda succinctly characterizes it as

> . . . a system of distribution in Indian villages whereby high-caste
> landowning families called *jajmans* are provided services and pro-
> ducts by various lower castes such as carpenters, potters, black-
> smiths, water-carriers, sweepers, and laundrymen. Purely ritual
> services may be provided by Brahman priests and various sectar-
> ian castes, and almost all serving castes have ceremonial and ritual
> duties at their *jajman's* births, marriages, funerals, and at some of
> the religious festivals (Kolenda 1963:11-31; reprinted in Dalton
> 1967:287).

Kolenda also observes that a *jajman* 'ritual service patron' usually pays in kind, based on the produce from his land, while the lower caste persons generally exchange services or exchange payments for services (Dalton 1967:287).

There appear to be many variants of the ritual service system throughout India and, additionally, a number of interpretations concerning the nature of this system (Dalton:285-332). In Kapileswar the ritual service system is more important symbolically than economically. No caste depends primarily on these rituals for their main source of income; only the Washermen and Barbers realize any economic significance from them. The real importance of this ceremonial system is that it provides a visible reminder that the Mallias are the dominant caste of the village and other castes are subservient to them.

The most important ritual relationship within the village is between the Mallia and the Barber castes. Both men and women of the Barber caste play central roles in Mallia marriages and funerals. For weddings, the Barber distributes invitations to the Mallia ceremony, carries gifts of betel nut to close Mallia relatives of the marriage party, and dresses and paints the bridegroom before the ceremony. The Barber's wife accompanies Mallia women and performs a religious ceremony for them at the shrine of the village goddess, located at the eastern corner of the village. Both men and women receive cloth for their services.

During Mallia funeral ceremonies the Barber shaves the heads of close relatives of the deceased, participates in a Mallia *shraddha* 'ancestor ceremony', and issues invitations to and cleans up after a funeral feast. The Barber's wife cuts the nails of close relatives of the deceased. Compensation for both men and women is in cloth and food which are given at various times throughout the year.

Additional castes employed for rituals associated with Mallia marriage ceremonies are: Astrologers (from Bhubaneswar), Potters, Herdsmen, Bauris, Weavers (from Bhubaneswar), and the Misra Brahmans, who also have important functions during Mallia birthday, funeral, and other ceremonies. Finally, the Washermen have the ritual task of washing Mallia clothes, which are supposedly defiled, after the funeral ceremonies. They also are ritually responsible for washing Mallia women's clothes used during menstruation and during the twelve days following the birth of a child.

Since the construction of the New Capital at Bhubaneswar, several castes have tried to terminate or modify their ritual service relationships with the Mallias. By 1962 the Washermen were commercializing their traditional occupation. Consequently, they refused to wash the menstrually stained clothes of the Mallia women, claiming publicly that it was too time consuming, but privately complaining that it degraded them. Because of new patronage from the New Capital, they no longer depended upon the Mallias for their income. This put the Mallia women in a difficult situation, for they believed that their clothes remained impure unless washed by the Washermen. They solved this problem by taking their clothes to a Washerman's house, dipping them and thus purifying them in his tub, and then carrying the clothes elsewhere to wash and dry.

The Barbers were less fortunate in their attempts to break away from Mallia domination. In 1962 they demanded higher wages for their work as the village price for a haircut was only one-fourth of that in the New Capital. Moreover, elderly Mallias expected a massage as well as a haircut. The Barbers threatened to move their business up to the New Capital, but the Mallias prevented them by threatening physical violence.

By 1971 the Herdsman caste had terminated their ritual service relationship with the Mallias, declaring that it was degrading to carry the covered litters of brides and bridegrooms at Mallia weddings. Since they sold milk to people in other villages and in the New Capital, they were not economically dependent upon the Mallias.

Attempts at Caste Mobility

Although the Mallias are considered a high caste in Kapileswar, their exact status is a matter of controversy. The dispute over ritual status is similar to those statuses described for many Indian communities. Some Mallias claim to be Brahmans, citing their hereditary temple occupation as proof, while rival Brahmans reject their claims. This involves what Srinivas calls "Sanskritization," that is, ". . . the process by which a 'low' Hindu caste, or tribal or other group, changes its customs, ritual, ideology, and way of

life in the direction of a high, and frequently, 'twice-born' caste"
(Srinivas 1966:6). A "twice-born" caste refers to a caste in the first
three categories of the *varna* system which undergoes the widely
practiced *upanayana* 'sacred thread ceremony'.

The dispute is not one-sided, however; for as Mallias tried to
raise their ritual status, Brahmans tried to increase their economic
and political power at the expense of the Mallias. Prior to Indian
independence, both parties were somewhat restrained by the fact
that they were tied to interdependent services in the Kapileswar
temple. The separation of ritual and secular leaders is widespread
throughout India. When there is a balance of power between the
two, it may lead, as in Kapileswar, to long-standing conflicts
(Dumont and Pocock 1957:I, 31-33; 1958:II, 58).

The starting point for Mallia upward aspirations was that
they worked as temple servants, side by side with the Brahmans.
By 1940 some Mallias had changed their names to Brahman surnames and had abandoned their distinctive clothes and caste marks
in favor of clothes indistinguishable from those of Brahmans. By
1960 the Mallias were claiming that they had the right to perform
the hereditary temple services of the Khuntia Brahmans. In 1963
the Mallias tried to change their sacred thread ceremony to con-
form to the ceremony used by Brahmans, but they were thwarted
by the refusal of any recognized Brahman to perform the ceremony.
In 1966 the Mallias took over the Khuntia Brahman temple services
by breaking into the Kapileswar temple kitchens, cooking sacred
food, and offering it to the deity. In the same year they held a
Brahman-style sacred thread ceremony for five Mallia youths.
(For further details see Freeman 1968:192-210.)

The Brahmans did not easily accept these encroachments.
Whenever they considered that the Mallias had gone too far, they
threatened suspension of their temple services. In 1940 and 1957
they carried out their threats which led to quick, although temporary, settlements of the dispute, since the cessation of services
affected the income of both castes. In the long run, it was the
Mallias who were most vulnerable, for they depended on the
Khuntias to cook sacred food which the Mallias sold to pilgrims.
Unlike the Mallias, the Khuntias were not restricted to working
solely in the Kapileswar temple since they had the hereditary privilege of preparing sacred food at the Lingaraj temple, the main
pilgrim shrine of Bhubaneswar. By 1960 the Khuntias had all but

abandoned the Kapileswar temple pilgrim trade in favor of better business at Lingaraj. This is what provoked the 1966 Mallia assault on the temple kitchens.

Curiously, since 1966 the Mallias have relinquished voluntarily some of their hard-earned recent gains. They returned temple cooking privileges to the Khuntias, saying that it was too difficult to perform the tasks of both castes. Also, older Mallias blocked furthur attempts to hold Brahman-style sacred thread ceremonies for Mallia youths, insisting that the youths return to the ancient customs. (None of the five youths who went through the 1966 Brahman-style ceremony have been able to find Mallia families willing to offer them daughters in marriage.)

In some studies of social mobility in India, it is assumed that groups tend to maximize their potential for social gain (Lynch 1969:204). In other studies it is assumed that mobility of lower groups is contained by the resistance of higher-status groups (Srinivas 1966:6). Neither assumption quite fits the Mallia case of voluntary relinquishment.

Caste Changes in Kapileswar: 1962-1972

Prior to Indian independence and the construction of the New Capital, the Mallias maintained strict commensality, touchability, and marriage regulations, with the latter the most resistant to change. In 1972 the only significant change from the traditional marriage regulations was the increase in marriageable age for both men and women, although a few Mallia women had deviated from the regulations. For example, three Mallia girls had married outside of Puri District: two because they were so poor that no Mallia was willing to marry them, and the third because it was discovered that she was having an affair, so her family quickly married her off far from the village to avoid further scandal. Also, between 1968 and 1972 three Mallia women divorced and remarried. The Mallias say that divorcee remarriages, as well as marriages of Mallia women outside the village, are new developments.

The Mallias have been somewhat more flexible regarding food and commensality rules. The ten-year period from 1962 to 1972 was a time of great changes in the diet of the Mallias. Wheat came into wide use. Chicken and eggs, previously prohibited because of their alleged impurity, were now eaten by the young men. They were introduced to these foods in the restaurants of the New Capital, where they took meals with people of other castes. Within Kapileswar, however, the old commensality rules prevailed, since Mallia women complained that their houses would be defiled if people of other castes took meals in their houses. Similarly, the women refused to cook eggs or chicken in their sacred kitchens. As a compromise, they agreed to cook eggs, using special utensils, on the outside verandas of their houses.

Some changes have occurred in the Mallia treatment of untouchables. By 1962 the Mallias no longer observed the pollution of shadows of untouchable castes, and they no longer considered it necessary to take a bath after entering a Bauri ward although a few Mallias did continue to wash their clothes. As a result of government pressure, untouchables in theory were permitted to use the wells and other public facilities in Mallia wards. In practice they rarely did so.

These changes came about through the abolition of untouchability in the Indian Constitution. The village school helped to spread this new policy by requiring high- and low-caste children to sit together. Although the parents of high- and middle-caste children resented this, they were nonetheless powerless to prevent it. By 1962 Mallia high school students were going to the movies with Bauri and Sweeper youths, and Mallia women, seeing them together, would call out jokingly, "Take me with you." Significantly, the high-caste youths did not mingle with their untouchable friends within the village.

In the New Capital section of Bhubaneswar the anti-untouchability regulations are followed, but in Old Town Bhubaneswar and Kapileswar they are yet to be enforced. To be sure, many of the grosser forms of public humiliation and harassment of untouchables have disappeared. The Mallias no longer swoop into untouchable wards on slight pretexts and destroy the houses, or tie the inhabitants to trees and beat them, as they did in pre-independence days. Untouchables no longer crouch and ask for permission to pass by the house of a high-caste person. However, in 1972 untouchables still did not enter shops or shrines in the Old Town area. They sat on the road and called in their orders.

Plate 12.   Because they are untouchables, Bauris are not permitted to enter village shops and tea stalls; sitting outside, they call in their orders and are served on the road.

They brought their own plates and glasses with them. Priests brought sacred food to untouchables waiting outside the temples. The Sweepers still participated in intercaste rituals which symbolically reinforced their polluting caste image. Thus, at an annual group ancestor ceremony, held each August at a small shrine near Kapileswar, after the high-caste participants had made symbolic offerings of cakes to the gods, the used cakes were thrown into the pond adjacent to the temple, where they were caught by Sweeper children. By taking the leavings of food of the higher castes, the children reaffirmed symbolically their own low status.

The untouchables know that within the village they will be blocked by the Mallias if they attempt to push postindependence ideals of social equality. Consequently, they intentionally avoid provoking incidents within Kapileswar, using instead the New Capital as the escape hatch for their new social aspirations. It is there that they spend most of their leisure time, seeking new, noncaste relationships. They go to tea and sweet shops and to the films, dressed in Western-style clothes so that they can mingle with people of all castes and gain what they consider to be immediate acceptance as equals in the new society opening up around them. For castes such as these, who do not own radios and who do not read books or newspapers, the films undoubtedly play a significant role in inducing rising material and social expectations. It is no accident that the wives of Bauris compete among each other to see who can get her husband to buy her the greatest number of factory-made cosmetics and other items advertised at the movie theaters.

Within the village, caste changes among the untouchables are no less significant, however. The Sweepers are Sanskritizing by changing their surnames to an ambiguous title which does not reveal their caste. Many of the youths refuse to patronize shops in which they are not permitted entry, and they have given up eating beef or pork, foods associated traditionally only with the lowest castes. Their elders have retained their old customs and food habits because they say that they are too old to change. But they say that they approve of the changes the youths are making.

CHAPTER FOUR

The Decline
of the Kapileswar
Temple

The Kapileswar Temple: A Central Institution of the Village

Throughout India there are temples which serve as regional and sometimes all-India pilgrim centers, provide a livelihood for many castes devoted to care of the deities and properties of the temples, and frequently have many social and educational functions (Aiyer 1946, Ramesan 1962, Stein 1960, Vidyarthi 1961, Bhardwaj 1973, Mishra 1971). The Kapileswar temple has fewer activities and simpler services than those of the great Indian temples. It is a secondary shrine in the Bhubaneswar pilgrim complex, and it caters mostly to local patrons.

Nevertheless, the temple used to dominate the economic, political, and ritual life of most of the villagers. Nearly three-quarters of the households of Kapileswar received some economic benefit from the temple. Several castes, headed by the Mallias, held tax-free paddy lands and tax-free house plots for their performance of specialized, interdependent hereditary services in the temple.

The temple was a center of conservative influence in the village. Prior to independence, Kapileswar was left relatively undisturbed, though this was not the case for many Orissan villages, for British land laws established in the nineteenth century led to widespread confiscation and sale of previously unalienable lands for nonpayment of taxes. At the same time, however, the British preserved the lands of religious institutions, such as the Kapileswar temple and other more famous pilgrim centers, such as Bhubaneswar and Puri, as nontaxable and nonsaleable (Hunter 1872:264-67,

49

Plate 13.   A full view of the Kapileswar temple.

273-74; O'Malley 1929:227-28, 233-34; Sahu 1956:395-96). This saved Kapileswar since its lands did not come onto the market. Consequently, until the establishment of the New Capital, the economic and political power of the Mallias and other tradition- ally privileged castes of the Kapileswar temple remained almost intact. The economic advantages of serving in the temple en- couraged the retention of hereditary temple occupations.

The villagers of Kapileswar pride themselves on being part of the larger, sacred community of Bhubaneswar. According to local religious tracts of the fourteenth through sixteenth centuries, such as the *Ekamra Purana*,[1] Kapileswar lies within the sacred space

---

[1] See Mitra 1963 reprint of 1880:vol. II, 110-18.

of Bhubaneswar. The boundaries of this space are supposedly marked by four branches of a mythical mango tree, with a trunk which reaches the heavens. It is said that this tree attracted Shiva and his consort Parvati, who subsequently moved their residence from Banaras in the north to Bhubaneswar. Hence Bhubaneswar is devoted to the worship of Shiva.[2]

The *Ekamra Purana* also provides a mythical origin for the Kapileswar temple (Mitra 1880:97). The story, often recited by the villagers, is that Shiva granted a sage three wishes. He used them to establish the shrine of Kapileswar, its sacred pool, and its custom of offering *prasad* 'cooked sacred food'.

Claiming that the original temple no longer exists, the villagers also can recount an origin story for the presently standing fifteenth-century temple. In gratitude for being cured of leprosy, King Kapilendradeva established a temple compound, managed by the man who cured him. This hereditary manager was an ancestor of the Mallias. The king developed complex temple services to honor the deity, and the castes performing these services were supported by the king's grant of tax-free paddy lands which became the property of the temple.

Within the sacred area of Bhubaneswar a number of shrines are considered related to each other. The deity of the key temple, Lingaraj, is designated the king of the area, and deities in other temples are considered his relatives and courtly advisors. The deity of the Kapileswar temple is called the chief advisor of Lingaraj.

This relationship is commemorated by an annual ritual in which the traveling brass image of Lingaraj visits Kapileswar. In

---

[2] Shiva is one of the most popular deities of contemporary Hinduism. He has many forms and is known by hundreds of different names, each associated with particular stories, symbols, and spiritual qualities. Shiva is known as the ascetic meditating god, the epitome of purity and spiritual control, but he also is known as the destroyer and the inhabitant of cremation grounds associated with pollution and death. One of the most frequent representations of Shiva is the *lingam* 'phallus', which represents the male creative energy of Shiva (Zimmer 1946:126). Such representations may be simply large, immovable blocks of stone, as at the Lingaraj and Kapileswar temples. In both temples there are also small brass anthropomorphic images of Shiva which are carried in festival processions.

return, Kapilanath, the deity of Kapileswar, visits his superior twice a year and, in addition, visits his own "vassal" village of Sunderpada once a year. He is accompanied by representatives of several castes whose turn to perform hereditary services in the Kapileswar temple falls on that day. On the Sunderpada trip, for example a Confectioner supplies *bhog* 'dry sacred food'; a Cultivator plays gongs; Herdsmen carry the covered litter; while a Brahman and a Mallia carry flat umbrellas. A second Brahman lifts the deity in and out of the covered litter and offers the sacred food. Another Mallia directs the entire proceeding as the villagers of Sunderpada greet the deity and present a symbolic tribute.

These rituals reveal the dual nature of the deity and his economic significance for the villagers of Kapileswar. In his anthropomorphic role as king, the deity is served by fifteen castes, in return for which they receive goods, cash, and paddy lands. As a sacred object, the deity draws pilgrims to the temple—an additional source of income for the Mallias who serve these pilgrims. Thus the deity provides a link between a sacred cosmology and daily activities in the village.

The Rituals of the Temple

Daily services at the Kapileswar temple continue the treatment of the deity as if he were a human king. He is bathed, clothed, fed four meals a day,[3] and put to bed at night. The major duties of deity caretaking fall to the Mallias and the Brahman cooks. A Mallia is in charge of the total daily preparation while, it will be recalled, a Brahman prepares sacred food in the temple kitchen and presents it to the deity.

Other castes provide goods or perform services when their presence is required; these interdependent, multicaste services reinforce the separation of castes on the basis of the ritual purity of the tasks performed and prevent alterations of the system at the

---

[3] The deity's meals of cooked sacred food—containing rice, lentils, vegetable curries, sweets, and curds—are later sold to pilgrims.

same time. The previous chapter indicated how both encroachment on the temple duties of one caste by another and improper performance of any caste's particular duties close down the temple as every other caste refuses to perform its duties, too. These work stoppages are effective in bringing about the settlement of disputes since closure of the temple is economically harmful to all the castes whose livelihoods depend upon service in the temple to the deity.

The anthropomorphism of the deity extends to annual festivals. All sixteen of the festivals held at Kapileswar focus on life-cycle rituals and other rituals of human activities attributed to the main deity or to subordinate deities. These include birthday, ritual bathing, marriage, and sacred thread ceremonies, as well as festivals when Kapilanath or his subordinates receive new clothes and special foods.

Only male members of castes are entitled to perform services at the temple. Fifteen castes are employed by the Kapileswar temple, though seven of them only appear at certain festivals during the year. Two Lingaraj temple castes, the Lamplighter and the Astrologer castes, also work at Kapileswar; while two Kapileswar castes, the Cultivator and the Nanda (a surname) Brahman castes, have nonritual services. The services, payments, and privileges of these fifteen castes are summarized in Table 4.1. Many payments are made in rupees. One rupee is worth about $0.35 at the 1972 exchange rate of 7.2 rupees per one U.S. dollar.

A total of 421, or 71 percent, of the households of Kapileswar have individuals who are entitled to perform temple services and receive temple economic benefits. However, many householders presently do not wish to perform their services; but at the same time they do not wish to be deprived of their temple privileges, especially their tax-free temple paddy lands and house plots. They resolve this dilemma by using proxies. A person who is responsible for a service on a given day supplies the proxy with whatever materials are required for its ritual performance; the proxy performs the service and takes home whatever daily remuneration he earns. The proxy system undoubtedly is not new, for there always was some provision for occasional circumstances during which people became polluted and were therefore temporarily ineligible to attend the temple. However, the present use of the proxy system, to avoid services altogether, probably is a relatively new development.

Table 4.1. Caste Services, Payments, and Privileges in the Kapileswar Temple

Caste	Number of Households	Services	Privileges and Payments
Castes with Occasional Ritual Obligations			
Samartha 'Lamplighter' from Bhubaneswar	1	Carries a light to the top of the temple during the festival of *Shivaratri* 'birthday of Shiva' in February-March.	One rupee.
Naik 'Astrologer' from Bhubaneswar	1	Forecasts events for the coming year at the start of the Oriya new year in February-March. Forecasts the deity's health. Determines the auspicious moment to begin each temple festival.	Small cash payments.
Bauri	100	Trims weeds in the temple compound. Also performs important nonritual services. Labors on temple lands held in trust by Mallias.	Small cash payments for weeding. Payment in kind for agricultural labor.
Barik 'Barber'	3	Carries torches during processions of the deity.	One acre per family of tax-free temple paddy land and tax-free house plots.
Dhoba 'Washerman'	4	Washes the clothes of the deity.	Temple paddy land.
Misra Brahman	10	Presents sacred food to the deity at the festival of the birthday of Shiva. Whispers *mantra* 'incantation' to Mallias at various rituals in order to purify a Mallia and entitle him to touch the deity—an important function both for serving pilgrims and for his individual prayers.	Two rupees for feeding the deity. Cash payments for whispering incantations. These are nonhereditary services; hence the Misras receive no temple lands.
Gauda 'Herdsman'	9	Carries the covered litter of the deity during processions.	Tax-free temple paddy lands and house plots.
Castes with Daily Ritual Obligations			
Guria 'Confectioner'	13	Prepares a sweet, consisting of puffed rice, sugar, and grated coconut, which is offered daily to the deity.	One acre per family of tax-free temple paddy land. Additional income from the sale of sweets which pilgrims offer to the deity.

Caste	No.	Services / Obligations	Payment
Teli 'Oilpresser'	1	Supplies oil.	Payment in cash.
Potoli Bania 'Betel Seller'	1	Prepares offerings of betel for the deity.	Tax-free house plots.
Kumbhar 'Potter'	25	Supplies six clay vessels for the daily services, three vessels for each festival, and additional pots for the Lingaraj temple.	Payments in cash, plus four *sari* 'woman's outer garment' per year for each family supplying pots. Additional income from pots sold to pilgrims.
Khuntia Brahman	13	Performs two main services: *suara* 'cooking' work (cooking and offering sacred food to the deity daily) and the *pujapanda* 'priest service' work (reciting ritualized prayers to various deities of the temple, involving the recitation of incantations and the performance of ritual gestures). Additional services: carrying the canopy which shelters the traveling image of the deity; and, on request, selling sacred food for Mallias.	The entire caste receives fifty rupees per year, plus tax-free temple paddy lands and tax-free house plots for each family. Also, one-fourth of the sacred food offered to the deity, and payment in cash from pilgrims buying sacred food.
Mallia	225	Makes daily offerings, including flowers and the food cooked by the Khuntias, to the deity; manages the daily services; bathes the deity and cleans his room; leads temple processions; holds an umbrella during processions. Also serves pilgrims.	Tax-free temple paddy lands and tax-free house plots; payment from pilgrims; receives back three-quarters of the sacred food they supply each day. Finally, Mallias have the exclusive right to touch the deity during personal worship.

Families with Nonritual Obligations

Caste	No.	Services / Obligations	Payment
Chasa 'Cultivator'	16	Acts as temple custodian, by appointment of the temple manager, to perform the following functions: managing the rotational system of temple services, informing people of different castes when their turn for service comes up, and sweeping the exterior temple rooms. Also sharecrops on Mallia temple lands.	One acre of tax-free temple paddy land.
Nanda Brahman	1	Acts as *purohita* 'family priest' for many Mallia families.	One acre of tax-free temple paddy land.

Total number of families: 423

Service to Pilgrims

Unlike ordinary days, when attendance at the Kapileswar temple is sparse, festival days draw large crowds of pilgrims. The Mallias have the exclusive privilege of serving them, assisted, on occasion, by Khuntia Brahmans. The main Mallia activity for pilgrims, the *jalasaya* 'watering ritual', consists of pouring water over the deity. This is said to "cool" the deity's poison. Occasionally, pilgrims from other districts and states visiting Puri and Bhubaneswar also stop at Kapileswar, but most pilgrims come from nearby villages, and certain Mallia families have the hereditary right to serve the residents of particular villages apportioned

Plate 14. Confectioners selling *bhog* 'dry sacred food' to pilgrims at the entrance to the Kapileswar temple.

to them. Often they visit these villages to distribute sacred flowers, water, and dry sacred food and to remind the patrons to visit the temple. They receive *dakshina* 'a religious present' for their efforts.

Since Kapileswar does not attract many pilgrims, some Mallias and Khuntia Brahmans supplement their incomes by working at the Lingaraj temple. Unlike the Khuntias, the Mallias have no hereditary rights at Lingaraj; however, Lingaraj priests hire Mallias to take pilgrims on tours and find them food and lodging. Some Mallias travel throughout India recruiting pilgrims for their Lingaraj employers.

Because there are not enough pilgrims, the Mallias and other pilgrim guides compete fiercely for the patronage of pilgrims, including stealing pilgrims from their rightful hereditary priests. O'Malley's description in 1929 of what befell a pilgrim who alighted at the Bhubaneswar railway station still applied in 1972:

> The priests . . . crowd around a visitor in order to get even a few annas; a score of them or so may generally be found loitering on the station to meet the trains, and they will run with the pilgrims for miles to secure their patronage (O'Malley 1929:266).

Prior to 1950 the Mallias blocked the road from the station to the Lingaraj temple and harassed the passersby until they offered some money. There were so many complaints about this badgering that the residents of Old Bhubaneswar finally put a stop to it; however, temple begging continues within the confines of the Kapileswar temple. The unwary pilgrim is often beset by four or five temple servants who cajole and threaten him until he increases his cash offerings.

O'Malley attributed aggressive temple begging to the relatively light pilgrim traffic at Bhubaneswar and the consequent poverty of the priests. At the northern Indian pilgrim town of Gaya, Vidyarthi claimed that pilgrim stealing and temple begging increased as patronage and income from pilgrims dropped in the twentieth century (Vidyarthi 1961:96-100, 105-09). Yet there is more to pilgrim stealing than economics alone. One Mallia pilgrim stealer proudly boasted, "There are those who hunt animals, but we are hunters of men." The recollection of another Mallia temple servant aptly characterizes the spirit, as well as the technique, of pilgrim stealing:

I used a partner. We would go to Puri and travel back to Bhubaneswar on the train with the pilgrims. One time, I struck up a conversation with a family of pilgrims. My partner remained in a different section of the crowded third-class compartment. The pilgrims told me that they wanted to see Lord Lingaraj. "But," they said, "our pilgrim guide at Puri was very greedy. He wanted too much money and we were very displeased with him." I replied, "Well, that is a shame. Perhaps your priest at Lingaraj temple will be better. What is his name?" They told me that his name was Gobinda.

Before we reached Bhubaneswar I told my partner about them. Because of the crowd, the pilgrims did not see me do this, nor did they ever realize that my partner was on the train. When we arrived, he got off first, then called out, "I am the pilgrim guide of the priest Gobinda. Is there anyone here for the priest Gobinda?" My new acquaintances cried, "That's our priest!" My partner came over to them and said, "Oh yes, I was told to expect you." He recited their names and home village. This convinced them that he was their real pilgrim guide. Then he continued, "My master, your priest, will serve you, and I will take you to his house, to all the deities and sacred places. But the priest needs some money in advance for preparations. He needs 500 rupees. Also, you must donate a bull. It is necessary for your religious duty."

This brought the shocked reply from the head of the pilgrim family, "How can I pay 500 rupees? It is too much."

My partner snapped, "Look here, you're just a little miser. You don't deserve to see the deity, you probably don't belong here at all. You say your father visited here, but he must have been very cheap, like you. I can see how much he must have revered learning. He certainly did not teach you our customs here. Do you think you can beg your way into Lingaraj temple, or fulfill your religious duty for nothing? No, the price is too much for you. You are less than a beggar. You are not religious, so why don't you go home? I will not absolve you of your sins, you - - - - - - - - - - - - !"

The pilgrim shouted, "I am not staying around here to be insulted and scandalized!" He ordered his family back onto the train.

At this point I called out, "What, are you going to leave Orissa without seeing Lingaraj, without being absolved of your sins? What a shame! But you do not have to do this. I am also a pilgrim guide. Come with me. I can show you Bhubaneswar, and afterwards you may offer whatever you like, or nothing at all. It is your choice. But if you go with me you must change your temple guide and your priest."

He asked, "How can I do this? Our priests are hereditary."

I replied, "This is a new era that we live in. You can choose your own priest. If anyone asks, just say that Gobinda used to be your priest, but he refused to take you to see the deity. Say that I am your new pilgrim guide who serves a different priest."

I finally convinced him. My partner left. The pilgrim and his family accompanied me towards Lingaraj temple. On the way, their real pilgrim guide met us. When he saw me with his pilgrims, he screamed, "You can't take these pilgrims away. They belong to me!" He ran over to me and hit me. Then a big argument developed. A policeman came running . . . .

Preindependence Temple Administration and Properties

From the fifteenth to the mid-twentieth century, the Kapileswar temple was controlled by a hereditary Mallia manager and his relatives in seven households. These trustees met to administer temple lands, enforce temple regulations, organize annual auctions for leasing temple property, and to keep track of the temple treasury. The cash of the temple was kept in the house of the hereditary manager, while the ornaments of the deity remained inside the temple.

The trustees also distributed rights to cultivate tax-free temple lands to the families of qualified castes (see Table 4.1, pages 54-55) who in return agreed to perform temple services. As long as these families performed such services, they and their descendants retained their hereditary rights to use the temple lands. Temple trustees rarely redistributed such lands unless the persons who held them died without leaving heirs. Thus many families in Kapileswar in effect "inherited" temple lands and also "sold" these lands to other qualified persons, and sometimes to unqualified buyers.

The lands administered by the temple trustees consisted of the original land grant of the fifteenth century, plus subsequent donations by individual patrons. The original grant included thirty-three acres of house plots comprising the central portion of Kapileswar village. In addition, temple land records show that the deity of Kapileswar owns well over three hundred acres of

paddy land near four villages in the vicinity of Kapileswar. Since
many priests do not report donated lands entrusted to them, the
villagers estimate that the actual holdings of the temple may be
more than double the listed holdings. The deity also owns properties which are leased annually. These include fruit trees, fishing
ponds, and small shrines frequently visited by pilgrims. The income from these leased properties is about 1100 rupees per year.

Each plot of land from the original grant was named for the
service or offering which it supported. Thus, the plot of land
termed *pana suari* 'betel preparation' was held in trust by a Betel
Seller family, in return for which they were required to present
a daily offering of betel leaves and nuts; the land named *sakala
dhupa* 'morning meal' was held by a Mallia family that was required to offer the materials for the deity's midday (late morning)
meal, and so on. Though many of the performances or offerings
for which the lands are named are reduced or no longer extant,
the records of these lands indicate that theoretically the daily
temple rituals required the services of nineteen individuals from
ten castes. But in practice, by 1972 daily services had been reduced to the participation of nine individuals from nine castes.

In theory, the temple manager was the religious but not the
secular leader of the village. Secular affairs were supposed to be
in the hands of nonhereditary leaders. In practice, powerful
leaders, whether hereditary or not, tried to control both temple
and secular affairs. Thus in 1930, when the temple manager was
strong, he assumed the secular responsibility of forming a pro-
tective buffer between the villagers and the outside world. When
an unmarried woman became pregnant and committed suicide in
the usual manner by throwing herself in a well, the temple manager effectively prevented a police investigation of the incident.
In this instance, the villagers approved of his action because it
quashed a public scandal.

Although most villagers in Kapileswar did not accept the
temple manager as a secular headman, government officials outside the village considered him to be Kapileswar's headman and
consulted him concerning matters of taxation, police control, and,
after Indian independence, election campaigns in the village. Even
as late as 1967, many years after the hereditary temple manager
had been removed from office (see the following section), political

candidates went to him first when they campaigned in the village, assuming incorrectly that he was a key man who could influence villagers to vote for them.

The Era of Government Temple Management

There are many reasons for the decline of rituals in the Kapileswar temple. One of the most important is temple management changes. Although British laws in nineteenth-century India protected public religious institutions from government control and also protected their properties from alienation, they also included provisions for the removal of trustees if they were suspected of mismanagement of their institution (O'Malley 1929:233-34). Although the public was extremely reluctant to take action against religious trustees, whom they viewed as the representatives of God, British laws provided the basis for contemporary legislation in several Indian states to regulate the management of Hindu religious endowments (Derrett 1966:311-36; Government of Orissa 1969).

In 1946 an educated Mallia court clerk petitioned the Orissa Hindu Religious Endowments Commission, the government agency that controls temples, to remove the hereditary Mallia manager of the Kapileswar temple on the grounds that he mismanaged the services. The court clerk hoped that the Commission would appoint him as the new manager. Instead, the Commission replaced the hereditary manager with a Brahman trustee from a neighboring village. This trustee, in turn, appointed a Mallia secular leader with a seventh-grade education as the new government manager of the temple.

At first the Mallias did not fully grasp the significance of the change in administration. They considered it simply another internal, factional dispute among Mallias, settled, as many were, by temporarily enlisting the power of an individual or agency outside the village. In 1950 the first government temple manager was accused of misappropriating temple funds and dismissed, so the Brahman trustee chose a twenty-one-year-old, strong-willed Mallia high school graduate (well educated by village standards) to be the second government manager. Within a few months he was beset with incompatible demands from the Commission on the one hand and his own caste on the other. The Commission proclaimed that the Kapileswar tank was temple property, and therefore the fishing rights to the tank were auctioned. The Mallias claimed that the tank was their own caste property; consequently, several Mallia leaders defied government regulations by fishing in the tank. The second government temple manager informed the police, who in turn arrested the leaders. Although after three years in court the case against them subsequently was dropped, the Mallias refused to forgive the temple manager for what they considered a betrayal of his caste and clamored for his dismissal. In 1954 the Commission dismissed him and, after two years of bitter wrangling with the Mallias, appointed a Brahman outsider as manager. Thus in 1956 the Mallias lost both their private trusteeship and all administrative control of the temple.

The period of Brahman temple managers, from 1956 to 1969, was an era of heightened conflict, deteriorating services, and demoralization of the temple community. Some of the conflicts between Mallias and Khuntia Brahmans have already been recounted. In addition, the Mallias split into hostile factions which prevented a unified stand against the Brahmans or the Commission, and resulted in the collapse of the Mallia *panchayat* 'village council'. (For further details see Freeman 1968, and for other examples of village factionalism in which outside officials become involved, see Bailey 1963 and Cohn 1959.)

With continual bad feeling between the Mallias and the Brahman temple managers, whom the Mallias accused of Brahman favoritism, in 1962 the Commission, to make matters worse, confiscated some Kapileswar temple paddy lands for construction of the West Daya Canal. Compensation was given to the temple fund, not to the temple servants and priests—both Mallias and Brahmans—who had been utilizing these lands. The response of two Khuntia Brahmans who lost land was to refuse to perform their hereditary services; others also questioned why they should continue their services. The Commission took the two Khuntias to court, and in a long, drawn-out, seven-year case it won the right to confiscate their house plots and remaining temple lands if they did not return to their hereditary service. During this period, 1962-69, the temple was rocked with frequent work stoppages, disputes, and violence, culminating in the year-long Mallia take-over of the Brahman kitchens. Finally, under the guidance of a well-known state political leader who lived near Kapileswar, a compromise was reached. The Mallias returned the kitchens to the Khuntia Brahmans; and, in turn, the Commission returned the management of the Kapileswar temple to the Mallias.

Declining Mallia Attendance at the Temple

What effects have crises of temple administration, as well as the expansion of the New Capital, had on the performance of the traditional religious occupations of the Mallias? By 1962 as many as 101, or 45 percent, of the 233 adult working males had abandoned temple work, and only 54, or 24 percent, depended mainly on temple work for their living. In 1971 the Mallias had increased their total numbers 17 percent and their total male work force 7 percent, yet there was approximately no increase in the Mallia temple work force, which remained at 55, or 22 percent. One hundred thirty-one, or 52 percent, of the total Mallia work force have abandoned their temple services completely, while the remaining 26 percent supplement their income with occasional temple work. It appears that the temple, with its limited lands and scarce pilgrim traffic, can support only a limited number of families; by 1962 the population of the Mallias had far exceeded this limit. Since only some 22 percent of the Mallias can expect to earn a living from temple work, the New Capital is important in that it provides employment for those who no longer can support themselves in their traditional temple occupations.

The slight increase in the percentage of the Mallias abandoning temple work does not show how greatly Mallia occupations have changed. The change is best seen by comparing the Mallias working mainly at the temple with those working as government servants.

While the number of those mainly dependent on the temple remained almost unchanged from 1962 to 1971, increasing numbers of commuting Mallias have been taking government jobs in the New Capital. This trend began in the early 1950s. From 1953 to 1962 the number of Mallia government servants increased from 3 to 34 men, 14 percent of the 1962 Mallia male work force. In 1962, 74 percent of these jobs were Class IV or menial positions. By

Table 4.2.   Age and Education of Mallia Government Clerks
Compared with Mallia Full-time Temple Servants in 1971

	Government Clerks	Full-time Temple Servants
N =	32	55
Average age	29	54
Average education (years)	11*	1.5
% illiterate	0	50
% attended college	50	0

*Final year of high school.

1971 the number of Mallias working for the government had risen to 63, or 25 percent of the Mallia male work force. More significantly, only 31, or 49 percent, are in Class IV positions. The increase in the number (32) and percentage (51 percent) of Mallia Class III clerks, including one Class II gazetted officer, testifies to the increasing educational level of Mallia males.[4]

The generation gap between the thirty-two Mallia clerks and the Mallias whose main occupation is temple work provides the most striking indication of recent shifts in Mallia occupations (see Table 4.2).

Government servants and temple servants differ in another important respect: attendance at the temple, which falls into three categories. The first, service to pilgrims, provides a source of income. The second, obligatory worship of the deity, fulfills an obligation in return for the privilege of holding tax-free paddy lands and house plots.[5] The third service, privileged voluntary worship, is performed for a person's personal benefits and has no economic significance.[6]

---

[4] See Chapter Eight; see also Taub (1969) for an account of upper echelon civil servants of Bhubaneswar, whose life-style and outlook contrast sharply with those of the low-level Mallia clerks.

[5] Mallia families rotate these services, and as indicated, if they do not wish to perform them, they employ a proxy to do them.

[6] This is a special form of worship open only to those Mallias who have participated in certain rituals which make them eligible to perform obligatory and pilgrim services.

Table 4.3. Percentage of Mallia Government Servants (Menials and Clerks) Who attended the Kapileswar Temple in 1971 ($N = 63$)

Activity	% Frequently	% Occasionally	% Never	Economic Value
Pilgrim work	0	28	72	Receive cash donations.
Obligatory services	0	6	94*	Retain trustee-ship of temple lands and house plots.
Personal prayer at temple	3	56	42	None

*46% of the Mallias are landless. Most Mallia civil servants hire proxies to perform their obligatory temple services.

Since working in a government office conflicts with being able to do pilgrim work, it is not surprising that no government servant relies on pilgrims as an important source of income. But they do have the time to do occasional pilgrim work as well as obligatory services and personal worship at the temple. Table 4.3 shows that the Mallia government servants have largely abandoned services and prayers at the Kapileswar temple, their ancestral shrine.

The decline of the temple is also seen in the abandonment and simplification of rituals, apparently a twentieth-century development. During the late nineteenth century, Kapileswar was a flourishing, though small, temple complex (Mitra 1880:58). The village was controlled by a Mallia shamanistic leader who directed extensive temple repairs and new construction. He also extended temple rituals by bringing Misra Brahmans and additional Khuntia Brahmans into the service of the Kapileswar temple.

By the turn of the century, however, the Kapileswar temple was floundering. Fragmentation of temple paddy lands through inheritance left many Mallia families with insufficient lands to enable them to supply the eighteen types of required daily offerings. Consequently, following a Mallia leader's proposal, the Mallias abandoned many of their obligatory offerings, setting a precedent which continued over the years. By 1963 only one Mallia family gave the full offering for which their plot of land was named. Similarly, the Khuntias dropped some of their offerings.

Equally significant has been the decline in the quality of services performed. A frequent complaint is that services conducted by Mallias are not performed on time, and this causes disputes because other castes are kept waiting. The problem of Khuntia rituals is much more critical. It takes several years to learn to perform their obligatory daily priest service rituals correctly, for the procedure entails memorizing exactly the different prayers and ritual sequences for twenty-six deities in the temple. Correct performance requires knowing the sacred incantations, ritual articles, tests for the purity of these articles, complicated gesture sequences, and offering procedures for each deity. This is about the equivalent of memorizing the contents of a 200-page book. Among the young Khuntias of Kapileswar, only two have received any such training; and they do not know or perform these rituals well. When the older generation dies, these rituals will die with them.

Between 1920 and 1972 there was also a reduction of daily attendants at the Kapileswar temple from nineteen to nine persons. Most of the loss (eight out of ten positions) occurred among Mallias and Khuntia Brahmans who abandoned rituals such as holding umbrellas, waving fans and decorative items, and offering items such as camphor and sandalwood incense.

Due to lack of money and interest, public participation in annual temple festivals has declined. Prior to 1930 the *Dola* 'Swing Festival', held in early February, was the occasion for five all-night processions of two temple deities, Kapilanath and a Vaishnava deity. These deities were carried around the village and, on the final night, to the neighboring village of Sunderpada. One of the highlights of these processions was the 'bull dance'. Images of bulls, twelve feet long and five feet wide, each carried by eight individuals, paraded and danced through the streets and engaged in mock fights. The bull dancers came from a cultivating caste which lived in two villages near Kapileswar. The Bauris of Kapileswar, similarly outfitted with large images, performed their specialty, the "king-queen dance." The Kapileswar Inland Fishermen, wearing costumes with wide wings that represented mythical beings, whirled about to the accompaniment of drummers and musicians. Hundreds of dancing and singing villagers followed the procession. In 1972 in villages a few miles away from Bhubaneswar the Swing Festival remained one of the largest, most exciting, and colorful spectacles of the festival year; in Kapileswar participation had been reduced to little more than a skeleton crew of twelve individuals performing their obligatory temple services with five villagers accompanying them.

Prior to 1950 the temple served as a center for religious instruction of the high-caste villagers. Teachers would read or chant
sacred books and then explain them to their students. This has
ceased; individuals who desire religious instruction arrange for it
in their own homes. Also, before 1960 Mallia dowries for prospective husbands often included rights to serve pilgrim villages.
Young Mallias no longer want this, and it has ceased to be a part
of dowries. The significance of these changes is clear: the Kapileswar temple is no longer a central institution of the village.

Flourishing Popular Religious Movements

The foregoing changes do not necessarily mean that the villagers of Kapileswar are secularizing or abandoning religion. Rather,
they appear to be turning to other forms of religious expression.
Since 1962 a few villagers have become followers of devotional
religious sects founded by various holy men. Other villagers participate in devotional ceremonies which are held in the evenings
in Kapileswar. Some villagers who never visit the Kapileswar
temple worship individually at numerous small shrines in and near
the village. Many villagers consult shamanistic faith curers for
help in crises. Women's rituals continue to flourish, such as many
forms of mother-goddess worship.

The one remaining vital feature of the Kapileswar temple is
a nonhereditary activity, faith curing. As noted earlier, the deity
of the temple is said to be renowned for curing leprosy. Many
patients go to a Mallia *kalasi* 'Kali-shaman' who performs his
treatments inside the temple compound. Curers such as this man
are found frequently in Orissan villages. Supposedly possessed by
the goddess Kali and thus imbued with her curative powers, Kali-
shamans may be either men or women, and usually come from
low or untouchable castes. Many of the curers participate in an
annual *jhammu* 'fire-walking ceremony' held in mid-April (K. Das
1953:49, 83-84; O'Malley 1929:84; Freeman 1974a:54-63). Although in 1971 seven Kali-shamans lived in Kapileswar, only one,
a Bauri, did fire-walking.

Nevertheless, fire-walking is widely attended by Kapileswar
villagers. Many of them go to the ceremonies held at a village located one mile away. With the Kali-shamans leading the way,

people of all castes walk the fire as a testimony to their faith
that the goddess Kali can cure them or help them out of difficulties. Permission to walk the fire comes from the Kali-shamans,
who remain under spirit possession throughout the day. In this
condition they are said to be the goddess herself. After walking
the fire, the Kali-shamans drink the blood of sacrificed animals
and then hold a meeting at which they offer advice and give cures
to the faithful. Their followers include high-caste, educated government servants as well as illiterate, low-caste peasants.

Each Kali-shaman is associated with a small shrine. A Kali-
shaman takes the local name of the goddess of that shrine, since
the deity of that shrine is said to have appeared to the Kali-shaman
in trance. These shrines are numerous. In Kapileswar, for example,
there are twenty of them, used either by Kali-shamans or by devotees with offerings. Although many of these shrines are in low-
caste or untouchable wards, they are frequented by people of all
castes. Several Mallia women, for example, perform daily rituals
at a shrine in a Bauri ward, believing that the deity of that shrine
has helped them out of personal difficulties. In the fire-walking
village near Kapileswar, a Bauri Kali-shaman has a large following
of devotees, from Brahman to untouchable, who daily attend the
shrine in his Bauri ward.

The activities at these local shrines represent a vitality which
is lacking in the reluctantly performed obligatory services of the
Kapileswar temple. Local shrines are used for many kinds of
ceremonies and personal religious expressions. One of the most
interesting shrines of Kapileswar is devoted to the *trinath mela*
'Three Lords Festival', an intercaste devotional songfest at which
the devotees worship the Three Lords, share sacred food, and
smoke hemp. Three Lords is comprised of three deities in one
image: Brahma, who represents creation; Vishnu, who represents
preservation of the world; and Shiva, who represents destruction.
The worship of Three Lords is considered a form of diversion as
well as a religious ritual. Although previously worshipped inside
the house, since 1950 the worship of Three Lords has become a
public spectacle performed at shrines and front verandas of houses
throughout the Bhubaneswar area.

In 1960 the Mallia leader of one of these Three Lords parties
constructed a small shrine a few feet from the front entrance of
the Kapileswar temple. On an auspicious day, the image of Three

Plate 15.   Singing at the *trinath mela* 'Three Lords Festival'.

Lords was installed in the new shrine and "brought to life" by a
Misra Brahman who recited the sacred *sanjibani mantra* 'life-giving
incantation'. A great feast, cooked by Brahmans, was arranged,
to which all Brahman and Mallia families were invited. Since that
time, daily rituals have been performed before this deity. In
addition, each year the birthday of the installation of this deity is
commemorated with an intercaste feast. What began as a form of
entertainment ended up as a tradition.

Another new development for Bhubaneswar is the dramatic
rise of *Durga Puja* 'Durga Festival' activities. The festival of the
goddess Durga, which occurs usually in late September or early
October, is one of the most important festivals of the state of
Bengal and its principal city, Calcutta. It is also widely celebrated
in the Orissan city of Cuttack. In 1950 and in 1962 Durga Festival was a small celebration in Bhubaneswar, attended primarily by

Plate 16.   A neighborhood display for the *Durga puja* 'Durga Festival'. The representation is not that of Durga, but of *Narasingh* 'man lion', a form of the god Vishnu.

a few Bengali residents. The villagers of Kapileswar did not celebrate the festival because they believed that Kali, their patron goddess, would resent it and punish them.

By 1971 Durga Festival in Bhubaneswar had become one of the big events of the festival year. Throughout the Old Town and the New Capital, residents had built large cement-roofed enclosures of three walls and one open side. Images depicting events in the life of the goddess were constructed inside these enclosures. Over twenty neighborhoods in the Old Town built displays and entered them in a competition which was judged by a leading resident of the Old Town. Kapileswar's Inland Fisherman ward, which is adjacent to the Old Town and lies outside the traditional boundaries of the village, was the only ward of Kapileswar that competed.

One of the promoters of this festival in the Old Town was a young, college-educated Brahman—a native of Old Bhubaneswar—who owns and runs a successful printing shop in the Old Town. Since his first shop was located in the Inland Fisherman's ward, he became their patron and the organizer of their neighborhood display. In 1967, through his efforts, money was collected and a three-walled enclosure built, an artisan from Cuttack was hired to construct a tableau, priests were hired to perform religious services, and musicians were hired to entertain the worshippers. Other organizers, most of whom were businessmen, started similar projects in other Old Town neighborhoods.

Without the support of the businessmen, the Durga Festival celebrations would not have grown as rapidly as they did. The growth of the festival also benefited the businessmen, for not only did they become respected patrons of religion, but they also gained for themselves additional customers from the large festival crowd.

In 1971 the Inland Fisherman ward families spent over 600 rupees to cover the expenses of their Durga Festival celebration. This amounted to some 25 rupees per family, or about a week's earnings for an adult. The main expense was hiring the artisan to construct and paint the tableau, which was made of clay. He chose as his theme the widely known story of Durga overcoming Bhimsen, the demon. The artisan worked for about a month to complete the project. At the appointed day and auspicious moment, which was published in the annual astrological calendar, a Brahman uttered the sacred incantations which were said to bring the spirit of the deity into the clay image. Then he worshipped the deity and presented offerings of food. This must be done each day that the spirit is said to remain in the image. Dozens of worshipers watched the opening ceremony of the celebration, and then presented their own individual prayers.

During the next three days, the Brahman and the people of the Inland Fisherman's ward worshipped the deity. On the third night, the inhabitants of this ward held an all-night celebration which included a feast and a special musical performance called the horse dance. An hour before dawn, worshippers prayed to the deity for the last time. Then the men loaded the images onto

a bullock cart and proceeded into the Old Town accompanied
by a raucous band and cheering, dancing attendants. Despite
the early hour, the streets were lined with worshippers who pros-
trated themselves or bowed with folded hands as the images passed by them. On the main road next to the Lingaraj temple,
worshipers carrying deities were streaming in from all parts of
the Old Town. As drummers played, dancers dressed as bulls and
horses leaped and twirled, careening into the crowd. Spectators
joined them, dancing and singing, swaying past the line of deities.
The dancing continued for several hours, until the sun was high.
Then the carts carrying the deities were dragged about one-half
of a mile out of the Old Town to a bridge over a small river.
The displays were dismantled, and the images were thrown into
the water below. After immersion, the images no longer were
considered to have the spirit of the deity within them. They were
simply floating, broken statues of painted clay which children
scrambled to carry off as souvenirs.

The appeal of this ceremony is not hard to find. The Inland
Fishermen say that they perform the Durga Festival for entertainment. While it is a religious ceremony, it also is a lot of fun.
The entire neighborhood takes part in organizing their festival;
there is something for everyone to do; there is the excitement of
competition and of pride in creating the new display; there are
special entertainments and special foods for the occasion, and the
revelry of dancing and singing in the final procession that marks
the end of the ceremony.

CHAPTER FIVE

Occupational Changes among Privileged Mallias and Exploited Bauris

---

Mallia Occupational Diversification

As indicated in Chapter Four, between 1953 and 1971 the number of Mallias holding government jobs in the New Capital rose from three to sixty-three. By 1971, 25 percent of the adult Mallia males were working for the government. The rapid rise of education among the Mallias is largely attributable to their desire to prepare themselves or their sons for government service, which they consider prestigious employment (see also Freeman 1971:1-12).

In the mid-1960s, however, as the growth of the new city slowed down, government jobs in Bhubaneswar became scarce and very difficult to secure. This is reflected in Mallia employment statistics: between 1960 and 1965, thirty-three out of the sixty-three Mallia government workers were appointed to their jobs; but from 1966 to 1971, only fourteen Mallias received appointments.

Mallias with high school and college educations are now turning to other means of employment, such as founding small food stores and tea shops. Although not as highly regarded as government service, running a tea shop appeals to the Mallias because it is an extension of their identities as high-caste temple priests who distribute sacred food to pilgrims. Prior to 1950 there were eight Mallia shops, six in the village and two in the Old Town. By 1971 the Mallias had founded an additional twenty-nine permanent shops though seven of them failed, usually for want of capital for extending loans. Table 5.1 shows the locations and dates of shops founded by Mallias residing in Kapileswar.

Table 5.1.   Locations and Dates of Shops Founded
by Mallias Residing in Kapileswar

	Village	Old Town	New Capital	Totals
Before 1950	6	2	0	8
1950-1962	4	2	1*	7
1963-1971	15	5	2	22
Totals	25	9	3	37

*Not included in the table is one grocery shop founded in 1955 by a Mallia household which resides in the New Capital. This household is also not included in my census of Kapileswar.

The preponderance of Mallia shops in the village rather than in the Old Town or New Capital is not accidental. It costs less to establish a shop in the village; frequently the Mallias convert a front room of their house into a shop. Furthermore, at least until recently, the risk as well as the competition is not as great as in the New Capital. True, the profits in Kapileswar do not match those of the New Capital, but the villagers earning income from the New Capital now have cash, and they spend it in the village. This is amply demonstrated by the rapid proliferation of food stores and tea shops in Kapileswar, which show a growth rate far exceeding the population growth rate of the village. Prior to 1950 there were no tea shops in the village. By 1971 there were fourteen village tea shops, of which nine were owned by Mallias. Since 1960 ten food stores were founded in Kapileswar, five of them by Mallias. Thus, a shop in Kapileswar enables an owner to have the best of both worlds; he benefits from the New Capital without having to leave his relatives, his friends, and sometimes even his own house.

Like most middle- and low-income Indians whose work is often seasonal, the Mallias show considerable diversity in their sources of income, for one or more individuals of a household may be engaged in as many as five or six different jobs. Well-educated Mallias who work as civil servants often provide the capital for other members of their household to start small shops. A Mallia who establishes a small shop usually does so in order to supplement his household's main sources of income. Mallia small shops rarely earn enough to maintain a single household but usefully contribute to the support of large households with several adult earners, in which shared costs reduce expenditures. Thirty of the thirty-seven shops founded by Mallias are tea shops, small grocery stores, or betel stalls, which require a relatively small capital outlay of from 250 rupees to 1000 rupees and which usually return a very small profit. Most surviving Mallia shops in the village are only minimally successful.

Another business enterprise of the Mallias is selling rice and vegetables in the markets of the Old Town and the New Capital. For the most part, the Mallias sell daily produce from their own lands. Like the shop owners, the Mallia market sellers have not had much success. In fact, their number has declined in the past decade. Prior to 1960 there were only five Mallia market sellers. In a rush of enthusiasm in the early 1960s, thirteen additional Mallias became market sellers; but by 1969 five of these thirteen had failed. Such a sobering business lesson has prevented any other Mallias from venturing into the market since the mid-1960s. Despite their interest in business, the Mallias simply do not have the business background of castes like Oilpressers (see Chapter Six for a comparison of Mallia and Oilpresser business practices).

Because of increased competition outside the village, the Mallia business failure rate is greater for businesses established outside Kapileswar: 33 percent for shops outside the village (four out of twelve) and 28 percent for daily market businesses (five out of eighteen), but only 13 percent for shops within the village (three out of twenty-five). Ten of the twelve failures have occurred since 1963.

Mallia Caste Tradition and Neglected Opportunities

It is as important to consider the opportunities which a group misses or neglects as well as those which it selects. The Mallias, like many other castes, reject many opportunities for earning which other castes of Kapileswar are utilizing. The Mallias, claiming that they are Brahmans, typically reject those jobs which they think would damage their prestige. This explains the virtual absence of Mallias in such previously highly profitable jobs as transporting quarry stones to building projects in the New Capital, skilled masonry, skilled mechanics, and crafts like carpentry, as well as less remunerative jobs like unskilled construction work. All of these jobs are considered hard physical labor and demeaning, since they require a person to work with his hands. The wealthier Mallia families have the capital but lack the mechanical and business knowledge to establish small industries.

Even in 1962, during the heyday of construction jobs, the Mallias avoided them. By 1971 the opportunities to earn from them had passed: the construction of the new city slowed down; quarries in the area became exhausted; construction contracts became uncertain; and both skilled and unskilled laborers found themselves out of work fifteen days out of thirty.

With the exception of one household, the Mallias also have neglected house rentals. People of other castes in Kapileswar, including strangers, have sold paddy lands and used the money to construct houses for rental purposes, which bring in substantial profits. Also, no Mallia has invested in bicycle rickshaws. In Bhubaneswar, bicycle rickshaw drivers pay owners a rent of two rupees per day. Within one year a rickshaw pays for itself, and thereafter it brings in about 700 rupees per year for the owner. But owners have frequent disputes with rickshaw drivers over the daily rent, and the Mallias, who view themselves as members of a prestigious caste, say that they do not want to be embroiled in daily petty squabbles. While the Mallias acknowledge that investments such as house and rickshaw rentals are good sources of income, they prefer lower risk but usually less profitable enterprises such as moneylending and investing in paddy lands. The Mallias have a strong attachment to their lands, which they refer to as their "food." Selling paddy lands, for whatever purposes, symbolizes to them a household in economic difficulty.

Mallia conservatism extends particularly to agricultural work. In 1962, 51 percent of the Mallia households owned land; but only 37 percent of these households worked their land. This number includes those who did all of their own work, including ploughing, as well as those who did little more than supervise other workers. Thus, 63 percent of the landowners did not even bother to supervise the cultivation of their own lands, sometimes because these lands are located many miles from the village. In 1971 approximately the same percentage of Mallia households owned land (54 percent), but the percentage of Mallias working their own land dropped to 31 percent.

That few Mallias work their own land is a consequence of their traditional religious occupation. They received tax-free temple paddy lands in order to give them an income which will free them to do temple work, a ritually higher occupation than cultivation. Consequently, they hire Bauri and Cultivator caste sharecroppers, so as to spend their own time collecting flowers and serving pilgrims. Paradoxically, the availability of new occupations in the New Capital also contributed to the Mallias' lack of interest in cultivation. According to the Mallias, a job as a government clerk or even as a low-grade government menial servant carries with it greater prestige, if not always more money, than that of cultivation.

Even the Mallias who cultivate their own lands appear indifferent to change compared to other cultivators in Kapileswar and other villages. Although their lands are considered among the best in the Bhubaneswar area, almost all of the Mallias refuse to accept high-yielding varieties of paddy, requiring new techniques of paddy cultivation, partly because of the additional expenses required to plant and maintain these new varieties, partly because the Mallias say that these new varieties do not taste good and make them ill. Other cultivators with less capital are growing the new varieties of paddy, are double-cropping, and are raising garden vegetables, which are in great demand in the New Capital city.

As indicated in Chapter Two, the Gangua River runs past Kapileswar; yet the Mallias do not use it for irrigation. There is usually abundant water in the Gangua the year round, although it needs to be controlled by earthen dams. Since 1955 the Mallias have not repaired their earthen dam; cultivators from other villages along the river irrigate their fields with the river's water. The only fields that the Mallias use for growing vegetables are about six acres located next to the Kapileswar tank. The water from the tank drains into the surrounding fields, making them suitable and profitable for the cultivation of *saru* 'taro'. The edible starchy roots of this vegetable are frequently used in curries. In 1965 several college-educated Mallia youths rented some dry lands and a water pump, grew garden vegetables, and realized a 100 percent profit on their investment. Calling a meeting and trying to convince others to grow vegetables, they received an unenthusiastic response; their elders told them to stick to traditional paddy cultivation and quoted an ancient proverb in support of their views: "Having no paddy is like having no father."

Unlike the Cultivator caste of Kapileswar, the Mallias show little interest in growing sugar cane or in keeping goats and chickens, despite the profits that can be made from them. The Mallias express their antipathy to keeping goats by saying, "Muslims keep goats; it is not our custom."

Mallia indifference to agricultural development is indicative not of resistance to new influences, but rather of selective adaptation of them, such as hiring laborers to work their lands while they themselves work for the government in the New Capital. As government jobs have dwindled, young, educated, unemployed Mallias have begun to reconsider the opportunities that might be gained by improving agricultural production on their own lands. In 1972 several educated Mallias began to work their own land.

Another area of little change for the Mallias is that of women's occupations. Like many castes, the Mallias prefer to keep the women of their households at home, where the women perform household chores and tend to their families. Women are discouraged from working, particularly when they are young, since a household whose women work loses prestige. Nevertheless, some women must work, primarily older widows who have no relatives or who are the sole means of support of a household, or whose income is a necessary supplement for an impoverished household. Of some 334 adult Mallia women, only thirty-one work for an income; all are over forty-five years of age, and all but one of them are widows.

Since the older women of the Mallia caste are illiterate and also have no knowledge of special arts, crafts, or new skills, their choice of occupation is severely limited. Like the men, the Mallia women sometimes engage in more than one job. Mallia widows have traditionally been encouraged to pursue some jobs over others. Begging is considered demeaning and is discouraged; pounding rice with a husking pedal is acceptable, as is distributing sacred food and flowers to pilgrims. Only three of the thirty-one Mallia women workers engage in begging, and only one Mallia woman works as an agricultural field laborer—another job which is considered demeaning. In contrast, nineteen women pound rice and fourteen women distribute sacred articles to pilgrims. The only Mallia woman worker who is reasonably secure financially is a moneylender who founded a food shop in the village in 1965. Her shop is patronized almost exclusively by village women, who also take loans from her. While there are many female small-loan moneylenders in the village, this shopkeeper is the only Mallia woman with a large moneylending business.

In summary, the pattern of occupational diversification in this traditionally privileged caste is characterized by great selectivity based on conformity to caste ideals associated with ritual purity and prestige. The exceptions, such as the seven men (out of a work force of 252 men) who are unskilled construction workers, come from families that are so poor that their only choice is to work at demeaning jobs or starve.

Bauri Occupational Stagnation

The Bauris, as well as other castes of Kapileswar, are responding to shifting conditions of employment in the Bhubaneswar area and elsewhere. For example, the construction of the new section of Bhubaneswar, with its many new economic opportunities, had the immediate effect of stopping both Mallia and Bauri migrations to Calcutta, and of influencing virtually every migrant from these two castes to return to Kapileswar (see Freeman 1971:7; 1974b:4). But how successful have the Bauris been in taking advantage of the opportunities offered by the New Capital? An examination of Bauri occupational changes from 1962 to 1971 provides a good indication. In 1971 the work force of 269 individuals consisted of 120 men, 133 women, and 16 children who worked full time. Many more children worked part time with their parents or collected fuel during part of the day. In this impoverished caste it is customary for women to work, and they do so without stigma. Most of the work of the Bauris is seasonal, and like the Mallias, the Bauris engage in several different jobs. Unlike the Mallias, however, the overwhelming majority of Bauris have retained their traditional occupations of agricultural labor and unskilled construction labor. Twenty years in an urban setting has led to some diversification of types of menial labor; but, with two exceptions, the Bauris have not turned to modern occupations requiring new skills (see Table 5.2).

Unlike the privileged Mallias, the Bauris do not deliberately reject jobs that are not prestigious. The lack of change in Bauri occupations is a consequence rather of the caste's poverty. The Mallias and other higher-caste people who own some paddy land can live off the land while learning new skills or seeking new jobs or educating their children to new jobs. The Bauris have no such economic cushion (see Chapter Seven; also, Freeman 1974b:1-20).

In 1971, 94 percent of the 100 Bauri households were engaged in agriculture. Five of the six nonagricultural households consisted

Table 5.2. Occupations of the 100 Bauri Households of
Kapileswar in 1971

	Traditional Occupations		
	Agricultural Occupations	Nonagricultural Wage Labor	Collecting Wood, Leaves, and Coal Cinders
	Households	Households	Households
Yes	94 (94%)	86 (86%)	90 (90%)
No	6 (6%)	14 (14%)	10 (10%)

	New Occupations			
	Using Traditional Skills			Using New Skills
	Selling in Market	Music	Transportation	Auto Mechanic
	Households	Households	Households	Households
Yes	16 (16%)	22 (22%)	7 (7%)	2 (2%)
No	84 (84%)	78 (78%)	93 (93%)	98 (98%)

of former cultivators who had become too old and weak or ill to
continue strenuous work. Among the 94 Bauri households engaged
in agriculture, only eight are owners of paddy lands, and their total
holdings comprise merely 3.5 acres, which provide only a small fraction of the food they need. Moreover, the quality of their land is
so poor that the owners are for all practical purposes landless. These
owners thus must also work as sharecroppers and wage laborers on
other people's lands.

Only fourteen of the landless households can afford bullocks,
enabling them to work as *bhag chasi* 'sharecropper' households.
They supply materials and cultivate an owner's land. Their share
of the harvest, which is 50 percent, rarely lasts them longer than
ten months. From the point of view of the Bauris, a landless
sharecropper is economically well off.

The remaining seventy-two landless households work as agricultural laborers, whose earnings of paddy are much less than that
of a sharecropper and usually provide food for not longer than four
to six months. There are two types of agricultural laborers, *kothia*

'farm servant' and *mulya* 'wage laborer'. A farm servant is hired
for an entire year as a full-time servant for his master. In addition
to cultivating his master's fields, he digs wells, rethatches his master's house, and runs errands. At harvest time he receives 12.5
percent of his master's paddy and straw, plus the entire harvest
from about one-tenth of an acre of land which his master lets him
cultivate. During nonharvest seasons, a farm servant earns two
rupees a day. Although a farm servant's daily wage is less than
that of a wage laborer, the Bauris prefer to work as farm servants
because it provides job security for an entire year with a guaranteed
daily income of food or cash. Over the period of one year this is
a much higher income than a wage laborer earns.

A wage laborer is simply an unskilled worker who is hired on
a daily basis for whatever jobs are available: road construction,
house building, agricultural work, and so on. When he is able to
find work, which is no more than fifteen days out of thirty, he

Plate 17.   A Bauri uses bullocks to thresh paddy.

Plate 18.   Untouchable Bauri quarry workers.

is paid three rupees a day. At harvest time, he is paid 8 percent
of the paddy he cuts. The Bauri women who do agricultural work
are hired only as wage laborers, who have no security of employment, and whose annual earnings are far below those of other agricultural workers.

Since 1962 there has been a decline in the amount of land
owned by the Bauris from four and one-half acres to three and one-
half acres, a decrease in the number of individuals who work as
sharecroppers from fifty-seven to twenty-seven persons, and an increase in the number of persons who work as farm servants and
wage laborers, from 203 to 230. Among the eight landowning
and fourteen sharecropping households, there has been a sharp increase in the number and percentage of their earners who supplement their incomes by working as farm servants and wage laborers
instead of working as sharecroppers. The increase was from 33 to
93 percent of the earners of these households.

The main reason for these changes is that more high-caste
landowners are dismissing Bauri sharecroppers to forestall new land
laws which enable those who cultivate a plot of land to claim it as
their own. The landowners, many of whom are not experienced
cultivators, now cultivate their own lands or hire wage laborers

rather than sharecroppers.   A frequent result is a reduction in yield per acre.

In 1962, 240 men, women, and children (89 percent of the work force) worked occasionally as nonagricultural wage laborers, mainly in road and house construction and at seasonal jobs such as digging wells and thatching roofs.   Fifty-seven men quarried stones.   (Women and children do not work in the quarries.)   In 1971, however, only 217 Bauris (81 percent of the work force) worked as nonagricultural wage laborers, including 182 who worked on roads and buildings, and 78 men worked in the quarries. Despite the increase in quarry workers during the period 1962 to 1971, the opportunities for work in the quarries have decreased as construction in the new city has declined.   In 1962 a man could find quarry work almost every day; by 1971 such work was available one out of every two or three days.

Women construction workers earn a daily wage of two and one-half rupees, while the men earn about three rupees.   Stone quarrying pays more than construction, but it is physically so demanding that only the young and the strong are able to do it.

Plate 19.   Bauri women working on a road construction project.

Workers are paid four-tenths of a rupee per stone. Usually they can cut about ten stones per day, or enough to pay them four rupees.

One of the major occupations of women is gathering leaves, grass, and bundles of wood for fuel. In 1971, 124 women from 85 households engaged in this task. Data on collecting for 1962 are not available, but data from Bauri autobiographies show that in the past collecting was an activity found in almost every household. Due to the cutting of forests around Bhubaneswar the women now must walk about eight miles to the nearest forest areas, spend several hours collecting wood, and then return with their loads of fifty kilograms or more on their heads.

In addition, young children and elderly or lame individuals who cannot work at strenuous agricultural and construction jobs, fetch fuel or collect coal cinders from the railroad beds. Others collect broken scraps of iron and glass which they sell for a fraction

Plate 20. An exhausted Bauri woman wood carrier.

of a rupee. Many Bauris sell these items in Cuttack, eighteen miles north of Bhubaneswar. They commute by train between these two cities. Instead of buying tickets, they jump on and off the train between stations. In 1971, 138 Bauris in 90 households earned all or part of their incomes from collecting fuel and other items.

A few Bauris have turned to jobs not traditional for people of their caste. In 1962 Bauris were already working as musicians; by 1972 twenty-two young men played instruments at weddings and dramas. Music making is considered an occupation performed by castes lower than the Bauris. But musicians earn five to ten rupees per performance, a tempting though irregular amount by village standards.

By 1972 a few Bauris had taken new jobs that no Bauri had held in 1962. Nine men from seven of the landowning or share-cropping households now transport quarry stones with bullock carts. The men earn one-third of a rupee per stone, and this amounts to seven to ten rupees a day during the dry season when the stones are quarried, which is two to three times the daily wage earned by unskilled laborers. In 1972 sixteen Bauri men, women, and children occasionally caught fish or collected grass which they sold in the Old Town market. In 1964 one Bauri rented a permanent spot in the New Capital market, where he sold betel. He also became a small moneylender. Within six months his betel business failed, due to family troubles which consumed his time and his capital. He lost his spot in the market, and now there are no jobs available. No other Bauri from Kapileswar has tried to set up a permanent market business. Three Bauris, all born outside of Kapileswar, work as bicycle rickshaw drivers.[1]

Most of the jobs which are new for the Bauris are traditional for other castes. Only two Bauris do work that requires modern skills; both of them are automobile mechanics. One of them was

---

[1] Bauri men occasionally reside in the villages of their wives rather than in their own home villages. This often occurs when there are no male heirs in a wife's family. A man who lives in his wife's village supports his wife's parents, in return for which he is usually adopted and eventually inherits the property of his wife's family. In Kapileswar there are four Bauri households with a male stranger and a female native, and I have classified these as native households.

a stranger who had acquired his skills in Calcutta. He then came to Bhubaneswar, married a woman from Kapileswar, and moved into her house. Subsequently, he trained one of his Kapileswar in-laws as a automobile mechanic and later helped him to find a job.

Comparison of Bauri and Mallia Caste Occupational Changes

Compared with the traditionally privileged Mallias, the Bauris do not appear to be making progress; for example, the gap in land ownership between Bauris and Mallias is great. While extremely few Bauri households own land, over half of the Mallia households do. The average size of Mallia and Bauri families is about the same, but the average landholding of paddy lands per family is vastly different: 1.37 acres for the Mallias, and only .04 acres for Bauri households. The disparity in land ownership accurately reflects disparities in wealth between these two castes (see Chapter Seven).

Clearly, the Bauris lack capital to start businesses or to get training in new jobs. The Mallias, however, can take advantage of new opportunities which the Bauris are unable to pursue. As we have seen, 25 percent of the Mallia male working force are employed as civil servants. In contrast, no Bauri has a government job. This is not simply a consequence of disparities in educational level, since many illiterate Mallias hold low-grade government jobs. In addition, many Mallias own shops, but no Bauri does. For the Mallias, government service and business are new jobs which have developed almost entirely since the construction of the New Capital. During the time of this spectacular development among the Mallias, the Bauris have been unable to break out of the cycle of low-paying, unskilled, seasonal jobs.

Bauris have few contacts who can help them get new kinds of jobs, including government jobs. The Mallias, on the other hand, inform their friends and relatives when low-grade government jobs in Bhubaneswar become available and coach them in how to apply for these jobs. On rare occasions, high-caste people help Bauris to find nongovernment jobs. The first Bauri to become an automobile mechanic got his start when a Brahman from his home village noticed the man's absorbing interest in mechanics and arranged to place him in a training position in Calcutta. Similarly, a Mallia supplied a Bauri betel seller with capital as well as with a spot in the New Capital market. But for most Bauris without patrons, these jobs are far beyond their reach.

The economic and job situation of the Bauris is dominated by the unpredictability of seasonal jobs, by periodic scarcity of food, and by mounting competition for highly prized but increasingly scarce positions as sharecroppers.

Since there are great disparities in income between sharecroppers, farm servants, and wage laborers, it is not surprising that Bauris compete desperately to get scarce sharecropper and farm servant jobs. They often give prospective employers gifts—food collected, fish caught in the nearby river, free labor—and much flattery and respect. The seriousness of their competition is seen when it is recalled that most sharecroppers are not able to get enough land to cultivate to supply paddy for their households for the entire year, while for farm servants and wage laborers, earnings of paddy from harvesting may last no longer than four to six months. Consequently, most Bauris must supplement their incomes by taking on additional jobs, such as thatching roofs, construction, and stone quarrying. These jobs typically are done during the dry season months of January to June, that is, between the harvesting of the old crop and the planting of the new crop. However, with a slump in construction and quarrying since 1966, dry season jobs are also scarce.

This is the condition of the Bauris under ordinary circumstances. As Chapter Two shows, during the frequent periods of crop-destroying disasters such as cyclones, floods, or droughts, the situation of the landless Bauris becomes much more desperate.

A final deterrent to Bauri success in seizing new job opportunities is that after centuries of social discrimination and economic exploitation, many Bauris understandably are afraid of retribution from high castes if they take new jobs. Thus the Bauris of Kapileswar have refused to learn to become skilled masons even though a skilled mason earns more than double the wage of an unskilled laborer. A caste of cultivators from a nearby village recently learned skilled masonry work and thus improved their economic standard. The Bauris, who work side by side with these masons, say that they fear learning the new skills—they fear making mistakes and then being dismissed from their jobs.

In summary, economic benefits from the New Capital favor high castes like the Mallias, many of whom have abandoned temple service in favor of civil service and new food business enterprises. These jobs are compatible with the traditional caste occupation of the Mallias as well as their images of themselves as a caste of high status. In contrast, the Bauris, limited by lack of wealth, contacts, and education (see Chapters Seven and Eight), are simply doing unskilled labor as their ancestors have done for generations. Obviously, economic opportunities have improved far less for the Bauris than for the Mallias. The result is a rapidly widening economic gap between the untouchable Bauris and the high-caste Mallias. By law, public discrimination against untouchables has been abolished, and in some areas of India and Orissa untouchables have benefited economically or politically from this (Bailey 1957:211-27; Cohn 1955:53-77). In Bhubaneswar, however, traditional economic-exploitative aspects of caste remain as strong as they were twenty years ago. The effect of the system is to channel the Bauris—men, women, and children—into low-paying, unskilled jobs, while denying them anything more than minimum earnings which barely keep them alive.

CHAPTER SIX

Occupational Changes among Other Castes of Kapileswar

Craftsmen: Potter, Goldsmith, Blacksmith, Carpenter

The Potters. The work force of the twenty-five households of Potters which are native to Kapileswar consists of twenty-five adult males and eighteen adult women. The traditional occupation of this caste was to supply pots not only for the people of the village and the Old Town, but also for the Lingaraj and Kapileswar temples, where pots used for cooking and distributing sacred food were permitted to be used only once. Thus, the Potters had to supply pots daily to these temples.

Potter women have always helped in preparing the pots by collecting bundles of firewood for the kilns. This is an all-day task, as it is for the Bauri women described in the previous chapter. The women also carry pots to the temples. All of the eighteen working Potter women still perform these traditional tasks; there has been no change in their occupations.

While most of the men (nineteen out of twenty-five) continue to make pots, since 1962 five men have turned to occupations that are new for the Potters of Kapileswar: one works as a low-grade government servant; two youths as printers; and two as shopkeepers. Unlike the Bauris, who are mostly landless, seventeen of the twenty-five households of Potters have some paddy land and derive either food or income from it. While they are by no means wealthy, many Potters have enough of an economic cushion to be able to afford to give training, education, or capital to their young men, who are diversifying their occupations. The most successful business venture of the Potters has not been the new shops, but house rentals. Two Potter households have houses for rent. One of these householders sold two acres of paddy land, built a substantial stone house with the money, and doubled his profit.

The Goldsmiths.   The previously well-to-do Goldsmiths have not been able to adapt as well as the Potters to recent changes. Nine of the eleven households of Goldsmiths who are native residents of Kapileswar are on the economic decline, as indicated by the sale of their paddy lands. In 1962 nine of the eleven households owned paddy lands totaling 15.5 acres; by 1971 only five households owned land, and the total was only eight acres. There are only two economically successful households: one of them founded a grocery store in the village in 1967; the other one opened a village tea stall in 1971.

The traditional occupation of this caste was a lucrative one; there was always a demand at marriages for fashioning new ornaments for women's dowries. Furthermore, the demand has continued—and goldsmith shops in the Old Town and New Capital are flourishing. The Goldsmiths of Kapileswar, however, have little or no business. Only eight of the thirteen adult males of this caste do any goldsmith work; the others are engaged in various unskilled enterprises, ranging from daily labor, to selling cigarettes, to begging. Only one male child is learning his traditional craft. Three Goldsmith widows earn a pittance in the prescribed manner, pounding rice or fetching water for other households. Although five of the eleven households still own paddy lands, no Goldsmith engages in agricultural occupations.

The decline of the village's Goldsmiths may have resulted partly from their inability to compete with the Old Town and New Capital Goldsmiths in creating new designs with high-quality work. Both the Goldsmiths of Kapileswar as well as the other villagers, however, claim that the main reason is that the Goldsmiths of Kapileswar were discovered cheating their customers and consequently lost business. One of the unsuccessful, landless Goldsmiths, forty-one years old, with an informal third-grade education and with no prospects for the future, described how his household declined during his lifetime.

Although my father was poor when he was young, he died a fairly well-to-do man. He began by making ornaments, but he did not earn very much from that. Later, he also sold gold and silver, and that is how he made a lot of money. With his savings he bought eight acres of paddy land. In his old age, however, he had leprosy and could no longer work. While I had learned how to make ornaments, I was not a good businessman; Father, therefore, would not let me have the capital to maintain the gold-selling business. He preferred to live off his capital, and so our business stopped. In order to live well, he sold five and one-half acres. At his death in 1963 I sold another acre to pay for his funeral expenses. In 1964 I sold one-half of an acre to pay for my sister's marriage. I sold the remaining land in 1968 to cover my own living expenses. The monthly expenses for my family (three adults and three children) are about 250 rupees, but my income is variable. During the month of May, although it was the marriage season and therefore usually a time of much work for us, I received no business. Often we starve; I have no money, and nothing to mortgage, so no one will give me a loan. When we are starving, and a person gives me gold to make ornaments, I often simply keep the gold. True, they get angry, but what can I do when we are starving? So you can see why I don't get any business from the villagers any more.

When I was young I learned how to cheat, using false weights, adding copper to the gold that people gave me. My father did it, my relatives did it, and I learned it from them. We used two sets of weights, an underweight set for buying and an overweight set for selling. We Goldsmiths used to work together to cheat our neighbors. Once, when I was a child and did not know about cheating, a Brahman friend of mine asked me to be a witness while his mother sold some gold ornaments. The Goldsmith who weighed the ornaments announced that they weighed two and one-half bhari (about seven grams). The ornaments appeared to me to weigh more than that; I checked the weight with my scales and found that they weighed three and one-half bhari (about ten grams). I was astonished. I announced that the other man's scales were one full bhari short. There was a great outcry. Later, the Goldsmith took me aside and said, "You fool! Why do you announce such things? You go back and tell them that the real weight is two and one-half bhari." I refused. Later, of course, I went along with such frauds. The Goldsmith eventually sold those ornaments as if they weighed three and three-quarters bhari, so he made a profit, through cheating, of the price of one and one-quarter bhari of gold.

This is how I learned how to cheat. But my family has been punished for it—we are without food. Most of the Goldsmith families of Kapileswar are in trouble; we have cheated the villagers so much that they no longer trust us. They go to the Old Town, the Capital, and even to Cuttack to purchase ready-made ornaments. They pay higher prices, but at least they get fair weight in these shops. The only Goldsmiths in Kapileswar who have a good business are a couple of strangers; they never cheated the villagers and their designs are good, so their business has increased.

The Blacksmith.   There is only one Blacksmith household in the village, and only one earner—a male. Traditionally, his main job was to make and repair the steel tips which were fitted onto wooden plows. Since he does not earn enough as a Blacksmith to support his household, he also works as a skilled carpenter, a job for which there is a great demand in the New Capital.

The Carpenter.   There is one Carpenter household native to Kapileswar and one male earner. He works as a skilled stone mason in the village, Old Town, and the New Capital.

Business Castes: Oilpresser, Betel Seller, Confectioner

In contrast to the Mallias, who have a business failure rate of about 30 percent, the traditional business castes of Kapileswar—Oilpresser, Confectioner, and Betel Seller—have fared remarkably well in business enterprises. The village contains thirty households from these castes whose members are native residents of Kapileswar. The men of twenty-three of these households established a total of thirty-four businesses which are still in operation—sixteen before 1950 and eighteen after. Several poor householders borrowed money to start their first businesses and were successful, realizing profits of five hundred or more rupees per month. Aside from widows, who are not about to run their deceased husbands' enterprises outside of the village, the closest thing to "failure" of any business enterprise of these castes has been the consolidation of two separate rice-selling ventures by a family which was initially running three businesses.

Most of the Oilpressers sell in the profitable New Capital central market, while the other two castes run tea shops, sweet shops, or betel stalls in the Old Town. Only four households have businesses within the village, and two of these are owned by elderly men with no children, who are not physically capable of running businesses outside of Kapileswar. Of the seven households that do not have businesses, two are headed by widows with small children, one by a man who is employed by a New Capital market seller, one by an old man who is too old and feeble to work, and one by a household that owns seven acres of paddy land and focuses exclusively on cultivation. Five of the nonbusiness households are landless. The business castes generally do not establish businesses within the village, because they consider the potential profits and the potential for growth to be much smaller than in the Old Town or the New Capital.

The success of the business castes is based partly on the fact that most of the households have the capital to establish substantial businesses; the business caste households are generally well-to-do and in some cases are among the wealthiest of the village. This is indicated, for example, by the correspondence between households that own land and those that are in business (see Table 6.1).

Another reason why the business castes have been successful is that, unlike the Mallias, they have the knowledge and traditions of a business community. Business for these castes is not a part-time venture but a full-time occupation. By the time a young man of the Oilpresser caste is eighteen years old, he has had several years of business experience at his father's side, where he has learned the skills of bargaining, selecting merchandise, pricing goods, and accounting; in addition, he has learned about the intricate system of credit relationships that his father has built up with his customers over several years or decades. At present, several of the young Oilpressers who have received college degrees are applying their education in establishing new business ventures rather than by seeking government jobs, which are not as remunerative. The Mallias, as well as other nonbusiness castes, are simply unable to compete successfully against this combination of experience, wealth, and dedication to business affairs.

Table 6.1. Business Caste Households of Kapileswar that Own Land and Businesses

	In Business	Not in Business	Totals
Landowners	20	2	22
Landless	3	5	8
Totals	23	7	30

The Oilpressers. Of the three business castes, the Oilpressers
are the wealthiest, owning an average of 5.37 acres of paddy land
per household compared to 3.25 acres for the Confectioners and
1.83 acres for the Betel Sellers. The Mallias, the dominant caste
of the village, average only 1.37 acres per household. Fourteen of
the seventeen Oilpresser households own land or businesses or both.
The twelve households that are in business own nineteen businesses—
two shops and seventeen market businesses. The four wealthiest
households of this caste own seventy-eight of the ninety-two acres
of paddy land in this caste, and have large moneylending businesses
in addition to their market and shop enterprises. They do not engage in any agricultural work. In contrast, the five least affluent
Oilpresser landowning households not only work their own land but
also work as sharecroppers for other households. Adult males in two
of the five landless households also work as sharecroppers. Of the
work force of twenty-five adult males, two females, and one male
youth, all but three of the males and the two females, widows who
fetch water and boil paddy for other families, are engaged in business activities. Among the nonbusinessmen, one is a government
clerk, while the other two transport stones to construction sites in
the Capital. While transporting stones might not earn as much as
selling in the market, the earnings gained from it are about three
times the amount that is earned by unskilled laborers like the Bauris.

The Confectioners.   Of the ten households of Confectioners,
eight own businesses and are landowners; two are landless, impoverished, and do not own a permanent business. The eight business-
owner households run seven shops, two market businesses, and a
paddy-husking mill. Of the eighteen adult male workers, sixteen
are engaged in business occupations and two are government clerks.
The two working widows of this caste help in business enterprises
within the village.

The Betel Sellers.   There are three households of Betel Sellers
that are native to Kapileswar; they have a work force of six males,
all of whom are in business. The men own and operate five shops—
four in the Old Town and one in the New Capital. Their shops sell
betel and miscellaneous items such as cigarettes. Although small,
these shops are well established and are extremely successful.

Service Castes: Barber, Washerman

The Barbers.   The three Barber households have a work force of five adult males and two adult females. Three of the men and the two women perform their hereditary ritual tasks at ceremonies (see Chapter Three) for which they are paid in kind. Two of the households have small plots of land (.25 acre and 1.5 acres) which the men work. These men also work as sharecroppers. One Barber male held a government job from 1967 to 1970; he was dismissed for alleged irregularities which are still under investigation.

The Barbers are poor as they have little land and capital. They are the only caste that has remained economically dependent on ritual service ties with the Mallias. Barbers from other villages have commercialized their traditional occupation by establishing Barber stalls in the New Capital, where they charge prices that are double to triple the price of haircuts in the village. Because of lack of money, lack of knowledge of new styles of haircutting, or both, the Barbers of Kapileswar have been unable to set up commercial stalls. In 1962 they tried to raise the price of village haircuts; the Mallias refused to accept this. The Barbers threatened to move their business to the New Capital, whereupon the Mallias promised to beat them if they moved their business. The Barbers remained in the village.

The Washermen.   The four Washerman caste households of the village are slightly better off economically than the Barbers. They have begun to commercialize their occupation (see Chapter Three) since there is a growing demand for Washermen as the New Capital expands. The nine adult earners of this caste, four men and five women, earn from 60 to 100 rupees per person, giving each household of this caste an income of from 120 to 200 rupees per month. This may not be high compared with the incomes of the business castes, but it is two to three times the income of individual Bauri earners and families. Washerman entrepreneurs from other villages have set up stalls in the New Capital; the Washermen of Kapileswar continue to cycle to and from the New Capital with their bundles of clothes.

Menial Castes

The Sweepers.   Of the three untouchable castes of the village—Bauri, Washerman, and Sweeper—the lowest of these castes,
Sweeper, is the only one which has made substantial economic
gains since the construction of the New Capital. What helped the
Sweepers was. paradoxically, their traditional caste occupations:
clearing the village of trash, cleaning out the latrines, and carrying
the nightsoil out of the village. These jobs were considered necessary, yet so defiling that no one else would do them.

When the New Capital was constructed, the city government
hired the Sweepers as the municipal trash collectors. Consequently,
all eighteen working adults of this caste, eleven men and seven
women, who are classified as menial government servants, earn a
steady monthly salary of from 110 to 220 rupees, depending upon
length of service and specific place of work. They are not dependent
upon uncertain, low-paying, seasonal jobs like the Bauris; they do
not live with the fear, as do the Barbers and Washermen, that if
they raise their prices, people will cut their own hair or wash their
own clothes. In fact, the monthly income of the Sweepers is higher
than that of many Mallias. The Sweepers may be virtually landless,
but they are wealthy enough to have one of the highest percentages
of bicycles per household of any caste of the village.

Brahmans

The Khuntia Brahmans.   The thirteen households of Khuntia
Brahmans own a total of 103 acres, or an average of about 7.9
acres per household. In terms of land owned, they are the wealthiest caste of the village. Only one household is landless: in 1962
the head of that household sold his land in order to raise the capital to start a cloth business in Calcutta; when it failed in 1967, he
returned to Kapileswar.

The traditional occupation of the Khuntias was cooking in the
temple, and men from each household of this caste continue to perform these services. The two wealthiest households also derive substantial incomes from rental properties in the Old Town and from
large moneylending businesses. In addition, however, six of the

sixteen male earners of this caste have turned to new occupations since 1963. Three of them are government clerks; two have established shops in the Old Town; and one sells firewood in the village. Significantly, the Khuntia Brahmans pay much more attention to agricultural development than do many Mallia and Oil-presser landowners. Six of the twelve Khuntia landowners work their own land, except for plowing. Since plowing entails killing organisms in the soil and Brahmans are supposed to avoid this, the Khuntias hire Bauris to plow the land.

In addition to the Khuntias living in Kapileswar, two village Khuntias with college degrees in mining engineering have moved to northern India for further work and training. A third college-educated Khuntia has moved to the Old Town and established a large pharmacy. In summary, occupational diversification among the young fairly well-to-do Khuntias is taking the directions of government service, skilled technical jobs requiring a college education, or new, highly profitable businesses which require substantial capital.

The Misra Brahmans.   Although they are higher in status, the eleven Misra households are not nearly as wealthy as the Khuntias. Nine of the eleven Misra families own land, but the average landholding for this caste is only about 1.4 acres. Like the Khuntia Brahmans, the traditional occupations of the Misras centered on religion; for example, the Misras were the family priests for many of the villagers. Three of the ten male earners of this caste work as priests. Another six are government servants— five of them educated clerks. One man works his own land, except for plowing. Two widows earn their living by pounding rice. Like the college-educated Khuntias, the most highly educated Misra, who is also a high-ranking civil servant (gazetted officer), has moved away from Kapileswar and now lives with his family in the Old Town.

Other Brahmans.   Of the three additional Brahman households whose members are native residents of Kapileswar, two are landowners. The three households have four earners: an old man who works as a priest, two young men who are government servants, and a young man who established a tea shop in the village in 1960. These households, like all of the Brahman households of the village, stress high school and college education for men, government service, and new business enterprises.

Agricultural and Fishing Castes

The Herdsmen. There are nine Herdsman caste households in Kapileswar with a work force of thirteen men and three women. All of the earners of seven households are engaged in their hereditary caste occupation of tending cattle and selling milk. The two earners from the remaining two households work as menial government servants, jobs which they have held since 1970. Five of the nine households are landless; the remaining four own a total of six and one-half acres. All four landowners work their own land.

The Militia. In Kapileswar, the eleven Militia caste households are predominantly cultivators. Although only three of the eleven households are landowners, seven of the households have workers who earn an income from agriculture: eleven of the seventeen adult male earners of this caste engage in agricultural work, including seven sharecroppers, and four are daily agricultural wage laborers. When they are not farming, twelve of the men work in construction-related jobs: four transport stones, three are skilled stone dressers, and five are unskilled laborers. The working women are widows who pound rice. The Militia have only one government servant in their caste, a high-school-educated young man who has held a clerk's position since 1969. There is only one business enterprise run by a person of this caste—a twig toothbrush business established in the New Capital market in 1971.

The Cultivators. Like the Militia, the traditional Cultivator caste of the village predominates in cultivating and construction jobs. Although eight of the eighteen households are landless, agricultural workers are found in twelve of the households; and seventeen of the thirty-one working males are engaged in agriculture. Ten men are involved in construction, including four who transport stones, one who is a skilled mason, two who are construction contractors, and three who are unskilled laborers. There are three

menial government servants in this caste; they were appointed between 1961 and 1969. One Cultivator caste man runs a village
food shop, which he founded in 1955. Prior to 1950 one Cultivator sold vegetables in the Old Town market. Between 1961
and 1966 Cultivators founded an additional six market businesses
in the New Capital in which they sell the particular crops they
grow. Two women of this caste pound rice for a living.

The men of the Cultivator caste are by far the most skilled
and innovative farmers of Kapileswar. They have experimented
with new varieties of paddy and have formed cooperative societies
for growing sugar cane and taro, which are good cash crops. Since
many of the Cultivator caste men are landless, they frequently rent
lands from owners and then experiment with new crops and techniques. Unlike farmers in neighboring villages, the Cultivator caste
men of Kapileswar have received neither financial nor advisory help
from the government. They learn new techniques by watching and
asking for advice of their friends in other villages.

The Inland Fishermen.   While the twenty-one households of
Inland Fishermen in Kapileswar have been influenced by the growth
of the New Capital, their adaptation, like those of some other castes,
has involved expansion of their traditional caste occupation. Members of seventeen of the Inland Fisherman households catch and
sell fish; twelve of them sell in the Old Town market. Prior to
1950 only five households sold in the market. Three of the four
households that no longer sell fish have men employed in government service. Between 1955 and 1958 three Inland Fishermen
were appointed menial government servants; in 1963 another was
appointed a government clerk. In addition to government service,
the Inland Fishermen are developing other new occupations: they
have founded two shops since 1963, one of which is a highly successful bicycle repair shop; two men have become printers; two are
skilled stone and construction workers; and two are transporting
stones to construction sites.

The Inland Fisherman caste of Kapileswar is by no means
wealthy. Only eight of the twenty-one households own land, and
their total landholdings are only about nine acres. But selling
fish in the market and going into new occupations have improved
the economic condition of this caste. Only four of the adult

Plate 21.   A Fisherman caste woman prepares pressed rice by pounding it with a husking pedal (right) and then roasting the rice on an earthen stove (left).

women still engage in the traditional arduous tasks by which they used to earn money—preparing pressed rice by pounding it with a husking pedal. It is hard work, considered demeaning, and is no longer an economic necessity. The new affluence of the Inland Fishermen can also be seen in the lavish displays they create at the annual festival of the goddess Durga, a festival in which they began to participate on a large scale in the 1960s.

Table 6.2.   Brahman Stranger Households that Have an Earner Employed by the Government

Type of Employment	Government	Nongovernment	Unemployed	Totals
Households headed by Males	22	2	1	25
Households headed by Females (Widows)	0	2	1	3
Totals	22	4	2	28

Strangers

Brahman Strangers.   The reason why Brahmans have migrated to Kapileswar is evident from the occupations that they hold. Twenty-two of the twenty-eight households of Brahman strangers have earners who work for the government (see Table 6.2). Of the six households without a government servant, three are headed by widows, one of whom is unemployed while the other two pound rice for a living. Of the three male households without a government servant, one contains an unemployed, single, male college student who is preparing to go into government service; another is headed

Plate 22.   A Brahman tea stall owner (a stranger) prepares snacks for her customers on the veranda of her house.

by a retired soldier who sells stamp paper at the court and helps villagers who are unfamiliar with court proceedings. The third household is headed by an illiterate, unskilled male laborer. Thus, twenty-two of the twenty-four male earners, or 91.7 percent, are government servants, a percentage that is far higher than that of any other group of the village. There are nine Class IV menial government servants, twelve Class III clerks, and one Class II gazetted officer. The only other source of income among the Brahman strangers comes from a tea shop that the mother of a government servant established in 1969 on the veranda of their house.

The Sea Fishermen. There are twenty-two households of Sea Fishermen in Kapileswar, with a work force of twenty-two men and eighteen women. Every household is engaged in selling fish, employing thirty-nine of the forty earners. The single exception is a male who established a bicycle repair shop in the Old Town in 1967. Of the thirty-nine fish sellers, all but two are peddlers; the other two are brothers who established a market business in the New Capital in 1969. The daily income from peddling ranges from 70 to 150 rupees per month per person, while the market sellers earn a steady 150 rupees a month per person.

Other Castes. The remaining forty-six households of strangers are from fourteen different castes and have a work force of fifty-two males, eight females, and one male child. Twenty-one of the households have earners who work as government servants, and fifteen households are engaged in business. Only seven households have earners who work in unskilled jobs, and only three households are engaged in crafts. The one child laborer is learning how to repair bicycles. Several households are engaged in more than one occupation (see Table 6.3 for further details).

General Conclusions

The data of Chapters Five and Six show, in the first place, that there is great diversity of responses to the occupational opportunities offered by the presence of the New Capital. The Mallias, the largest caste of the village, show the greatest diversity of responses.

Table 6.3.   Occupations of the Remaining Forty-six Stranger Households

	Number of Households	Government Service			Business			Crafts	Unskilled Labor	Other
		IV	III	II	Shop	Market	Peddler			
Scribe	8	3	1	1	1	1	0	0	0	2
Menial castes	2	2	0	0	0	0	0	0	0	0
Crafts castes	6	1	1	0	2	0	0	3	0	0
Business castes	15	3	2	0	2	3	3	0	2	1
Agriculture and Fishing castes	15	4	2	1	1	1	1	0	5	2
Totals	46	13	6	2	6	5	4	3	7	5

Totals:	Number of Households	Government Service	Business	Crafts	Unskilled Labor	Other
Households	46	21	15	3	7	5
Earners	61	23	17	4	8	9

Table 6.4.   Household Occupations of Six Castes Whose Earners
Resided in Kapileswar in 1971

	Number of Households	Number of Landowners	Average size of Landholdings (acres)	Unemployed	Religion	Government Service	Shops
Native Residents							
Khuntia Brahmans	13	12	7.39	0	13	3	2
Mallias	225	117	1.26	4	124	51	26
Oilpressers	17	12	5.4	0	0	1	2
Bauris	100	8	0.04	0	0	0	0
Strangers							
Brahmans	28			2	0	22	1
Sea Fishermen	22			0	0	0	1

In great measure, Mallia occupational diversification is a consequence
of variations in wealth and education among Mallia households: the
wealthiest have the highest levels of education and the highest percentage of earners in the clerk's level of the civil service; slightly
less well off or less well educated Mallias are in business; the poor-
est and least educated Mallias are in temple work, and when that
is insufficient for survival they do menial and unskilled jobs which
are incompatible with the status expectations of this traditionally
privileged caste. For the Bauris, the lack of wealth, education, and
skills is the overwhelming determinant of their limited occupational
choices.

But wealth alone does not sufficiently explain why the Mallias
and earners from other castes have selected certain jobs out of the
many that are available. Clearly, there is great selectivity by caste
regarding occupational choice. (Table 6.4 provides a summary of the
contrasting responses of six castes of the village.) Virtually every caste
of the village has used its traditional caste occupation or training as a
springboard for seizing new opportunities in the New Capital. The
overwhelming majority of the earners of Kapileswar—native residents
as well as strangers—retain strong ties with their traditional caste occupations or have adapted traditional skills to new situations. Many

Markets	Professional and Skilled Labor	Unskilled Construction Labor	Agriculture (Own Land, and Sharecropper)	Agricultural Labor	Sell Fish	Other	Collecting
0	0	0	6	0	0	3	0
13	0	16	43	5	0	48	0
10	0	1	7	0	0	6	0
16	2	86	22	72	0	28	90
0	0	1	0	0	0	3	0
1	0	0	0	0	22	0	0

earners are simply commercializing caste occupations with which they are already familiar: Potters sell pots, Herdsmen tend cattle and sell milk, Barbers cut hair, Inland and Sea Fisherman castes sell fish, business castes run businesses, Cultivators experiment with cash crops, Sweepers work as municipal garbage collectors, and so on.

From this point of view, the persistence of traditional caste occupations in the New Capital is the most striking feature of occupational selection and diversification. Even those who have changed to new occupations provide examples of how old caste traditions have influenced their decisions. The Mallia government employees, for example, work in the New Capital but live in their home village. They unhesitatingly abandon their traditional temple occupations, but not village life. Moreover, their choice of occupation fits their images of themselves as Brahmans, who for generations have considered civil service an acceptable alternative to religious work. Like the Mallias, the highly successful business castes are benefiting from the New Capital while remaining rooted in the old village. The adherence to tradition plus the fact that Bhubaneswar is an administrative rather than an industrial city, has helped to introduce new consumer expectations but not new skills. With the exception of the Bauris, who seem to have little choice, the villagers' selection of new economic opportunities is influenced by their attempts to accommodate the new opportunities to their old life-style and caste traditions.

Occupational diversification in Bhubaneswar illustrates the complexity of the adaptive processes of castes that are modernizing and urbanizing. Some castes, like the Oilpressers, the Inland Fisherman castes, and the Brahman castes, including strangers, have made highly successful transitions to the new urban environment while, for many reasons, castes like the Bauris, Goldsmiths, Barbers, and Cultivators have failed to adapt successfully to the new city. Others, like the Mallias, have had both successes and failures in adapting. Thus, sweeping generalizations about the adaptability or lack of adaptability of castes in urbanizing settings do not fit the situation in Bhubaneswar.

As the comparison of Mallias and Bauris shows, the wealth of castes affects the success or failure of their occupational adaptations. But wealth, or the lack of it, is not a sufficient explanation of why some castes succeeded in adapting while others failed, nor is it an explanation of some of the ironic consequences that have developed as a result of caste change and urbanization. Like the Bauris, the Sweepers were poor and followed their traditional caste occupations in the new city, but the results for the two castes were quite different: the Bauris have made no economic gains while the Sweepers are substantially better off. The reasonably well-off Mallias had the wealth to try new occupations like business, but their outlook as traditional temple priests prevented their success as businessmen. The well-to-do Goldsmiths destroyed their chances for economic gain by cheating. Despite their innovative approaches to agriculture, the Cultivators are hampered by being sharecroppers for indifferent landowners who do not care whether or not agricultural improvements are made. Like the Bauris, the Cultivators depend economically on higher, wealthier castes that try to prevent low-caste and poor people from improving their lot if it interferes with higher-caste life-styles and economic gains.

The directions of occupational change and the success or failure of urbanizing castes depends, then, not only upon wealth but upon fortuitous circumstances like the type of city that is growing up around them, what that city offers, and what it needs. The New Capital needs garbage collectors, but it does not need temple priests or steel workers. Since it is primarily an administrative center and not an industrial complex, there is an abundance of civil servants but a lack of people with new technical skills, a plethora of small businessmen who cater to government employees but an absence of small industrialists. The Kapileswar castes that benefited from the new city were those whose skills could be utilized or adapted to the particular urban environment of Bhubaneswar.

The importance of occupational niches is strikingly illustrated with the contrast between the Sweepers and the Bauris. The Bauris do not have a specialized hereditary caste occupation as do the Sweepers. The Bauris traditionally have done unskilled labor, but so do poor people across the entire spectrum of the caste hierarchy. Thus, at the time that the new capital city of Bhubaneswar was being built, unskilled workers were hired from many castes; the Bauris had no protection, and are now competing for scarce jobs with these workers from other castes.

In contrast, the Sweepers have a highly specialized occupational niche which is indispensable for the city as well as the village. Not only are the Sweepers assured of employment, but in addition they are protected from encroachment by the poor of other castes. Because of its polluting character, no one but a Sweeper is willing to work as a Sweeper. Thus the Sweepers are saved precisely because they retain their hereditary polluting occupation, thus perpetuating the stigma traditionally associated with their caste.

The case of the Sweepers shows that the economics of caste change cannot be explained without also considering the symbols of caste. The economic-exploitative aspect of caste, which helps to maintain the separation of castes, is matched by a symbolic system which is focused on pollution and purity, in which caste identities are carefully demarcated, and certain jobs and activities are ideally set apart as symbolic of different caste identities. The importance of the symbols of caste identity in influencing occupational change is amply demonstrated by the data in Chapters Five and Six.

If caste perpetuates differences, so caste itself is perpetuated by the ways in which the opportunities of the New Capital are presented to the villagers, are perceived by them, and are acted on by them. This does not mean that caste and modern urbanization are incompatible, but quite the reverse. The traditional and the modern are inseparable. The New Capital of Bhubaneswar is changing the village of Kapileswar and its castes, but in turn the villagers are making the city an extension of their caste-based village community.

CHAPTER SEVEN

The Distribution
of Wealth
in Kapileswar

Land, Wealth, and Income

There are three useful indicators of the wealth of households in Kapileswar: first, the amount of cultivable land owned; second, the amount of wealth owned other than land (other wealth); and third, annual household income, based on the average number of adults per household. In order to measure the distribution of wealth for every household of Kapileswar, I have used a nine-point scale for each of the three indicators, and a fourth cumulative scale which combines the measures of land, other wealth, and income (see Tables 7.1, 7.4, 7.5, and 7.6).

In Table 7.1, my classification of landowners into low, middle, well-to-do, etc., was based on the villagers' estimates of the amount of land that is needed to support a family of five. The villagers assume that ideally an adult male will consume between .5 and .6 kilograms of husked rice per day, or about 180 to 215 kilograms (about 396 to 473 pounds) per year. Adult female consumption ideally is about .4 kilogram per day, or about 140 kilograms (about 308 pounds) per year. Unhusked paddy is slightly more than double the weight of husked rice, so the annual consumption per adult is twice that of husked rice.[1]

---

[1] The Bureau of Statistics and Economics, Government of Orissa, considers cleaned rice to comprise 65 percent of the green rates of paddy (Government of Orissa 1972:4). Other foods with nutritional value are eaten by persons who can afford them (see pages 17 and 18, and Care 1972).

Table 7.1. Acres of Cultivable Land Owned per Household

Land scale classification	1 No land	2 Low	3 Low	4 Low	5 Middle	6 Middle	7 Well-to-do	8 Well-to-do	9 Wealthy	Totals
Acres	0	.1-.24	.25-.49	.5-.99	1-2.9	3-4.9	5-9.9	10-19.9	Over 20	
Households										
Native residents	266	3	21	31	113	36	21	1	6	498
Strangers	77	2	1	0	7	2	5	1	1	96
Entire village	343	5	22	31	120	38	26	2	7	594
	No land	Low (Under 1 Acre)			Middle (1-4.9 Acres)		Well-to-do (5-19.9 Acres)		Wealthy Over 20	
Totals	343	58			158		28		7	594

A family of five with one adult male, one adult female, and three children ideally would consume between 1300 and 1600 kilograms (2860 to 3520 pounds) of unhusked rice annually. The paddy yields per acre from the lands around Kapileswar range from 270 kilograms (594 pounds) on poor land to 720 kilograms (1584 pounds) per acre on good land. An average acre yields about 500 kilograms (1100 pounds) per acre, which is higher than the 1970-71 all-Orissan average of 390 kilograms (858 pounds) per acre.[2] Thus, in order to be supported solely by produce from average paddy lands, a family of five would need to own nearly 3 acres which they personally cultivate. A single adult needs about .7 acre to survive. The villagers' estimate is close to that of Sinha's, who estimates that in the coastal plains of Orissa, a holding of 1.2 hectare (2.47 acres) is the minimum size necessary to support a family of five (Sinha 1971:58). Misra estimates that in the coastal plains the minimum acreage necessary for a family to survive is about 3.5 acres (Misra 1961:110-11). In the district of Puri, where Kapileswar is located, the average size plot is about .3 acre.

In Kapileswar, only 63 out of 594 households, or 10.6 percent, own enough paddy land to be supported solely by their lands (see Table 7.2). This is one reason why there is such wide occupational diversification as well as multiple job holding by the people of Kapileswar.

Table 7.2.   Households Owning Above and Below the Land Survival Figure of .7 Acre per Adult (3 Acres per 5-Member Household)

	Native Residents		Strangers		Entire Village	
	Number of Households	%	Number of Households	%	Number of Households	%
Above	54	(11)	9	(9.4)	63	(10.6)
Below	444	(89)	87	(90.6)	531	(89.4)
Totals	498	(100)	96	(100)	594	(100)

---

[2] The average yield in Orissa in 1970-71 was 960 kilograms per hectare (2.47 acres), or about 390 kilograms per acre. This is a decline from the 1963-64 yield of 1000 kilograms per hectare, and is less than the all-India average (Care 1972:46-47; Sinha 1971:56-58: Stat. Section Orissa 1970-71).

Sinha observes that inequality in land ownership is quite noticeable in Orissa, since ". . . less than 20 percent of the land-holders (with more than 8 hectares of land [about 20 acres]) account for 60 percent of the total land of the state. The rest of 39.9 percent of the land is owned by more than 80 percent of peasants" (Sinha 1971:58).

In Kapileswar, as in Orissa generally, land inequalities are quite pronounced. At the bottom of the scale there is a large landless population that comprises nearly 60 percent of Kapiles-war's households, while at the other extreme, about 1 percent of the households own nearly 30 percent of the land. The largest number of acres owned is among owners of middle size plots (see Table 7.3).

Table 7.3. Total Acres Owned by Landowners
of Different Size Holdings

Acres	Number of Households	%	Number of Acres Owned	%
Landless	343	(57.5)	0	(0)
Under 1 acre	58	(9.8)	24.53	(3.1)
1.0-4.9 acres	158	(26.6)	335.43	(43.1)
5.0-9.9 acres	26	(4.4)	166.50	(21.2)
10.0-19.9 acres	2	(.3)	28.0	(3.6)
20 acres and up	7	(1.2)	223.0	(28.9)
Totals	594	(100.0)	777.46	(99.9)
Average size landholding:		1.30 acres		

As shown in Table 7.4, households in Kapileswar range from homeless beggars and widows who own virtually nothing, to house-holds whose wealth other than land exceeds 100,000 rupees, or over U.S. $13,000, and who own many new luxury items.

Strangers own a higher percentage of most luxury items than do native residents. This reflects the high number of relatively well-off strangers who work as civil servants or who have businesses or professional occupations in the New Capital. The strangers keep little livestock. Most of them do no cultivation, and many of those who rent have no room for animals nor time to care for them.

Table 7.4.   Wealth Owned Other Than Land per Household *

Wealth scale	1	2	3	4	5	6	7	8	9	Totals
Classification	Very low	Very low	Low	Low	Middle	Middle	Well-to-do	Well-to-do	Wealthy	
Rupee value	0-99	100-499	500-999	1000-4999	5000-9999	10,000-19,999	20,000-49,999	50,000-99,999	100,000 and up	
Households										
Native residents	5	162	109	133	37	28	16	4	4	498
Strangers	12	49	13	14	3	1	2	1	1	96
Entire village	17	211	121	148	40	29	18	5	5	594
Rupees	Very low (0-499)		Low (500-4999)		Middle (5000-19,999)		Well-to-do (20,000-99,999)		Wealthy (100,000+)	
Totals	288		269		69		23		5	594

* The figures used in the above table are based on estimates of the value of such items as houses, evaluated in terms of the number of rooms, whether built of stone or mud, and whether built with stone, metal, tile, or thatch roofs; income property other than paddy lands; luxury items like bicycles, wristwatches, radios, electricity, running water; implements like plows and carts; and numbers and kinds of livestock. Jewelry was not included because it was not possible to estimate the amount or value per household.

Table 7.5. Annual Income per Household Based on Average Number of Adults per Household*

Income scale	1	2	3	4	5	6	7	8	9	Totals
Classification	Starvation		Low	Middle	Middle	Well-to-do		Wealthy	Wealthy	
Rupee value	Under 125	125-249	250-499	500-749	750-999	1000-1749	1750-2499	2500-4999	5000 and up	
Households										
Native residents	6	22	178	143	51	78	14	6	0	498
Strangers	1	3	28	23	12	17	7	4	1	96
Entire village	7	25	206	166	63	95	21	10	1	594
	Starvation		Low	Middle		Well-to-do		Wealthy		
Rupees	(0-249)		(250-499)	(500-999)		(1000-2499)		(2500 and up)		
Totals	32		206	229		116		11		594

*This table shows the annual income per household, based on the average number of adults per household. An adult is defined as anyone who is 15 years of age or older; children are considered as follows: ages 10-14 = .75 adult; ages 2-9 = .5 adult; children under 2 = .25 adult. Thus a household of 2 adults and 3 children whose ages are 5, 9, and 12 are considered equivalent to 3.75 adults.

A determination of annual household income on this basis makes possible an estimate of how many households earn an income which is below the subsistence level for an average adult.

Table 7.5 shows the annual income per household, based on the average number of adults per household. In Bhubaneswar in 1971 an adult could barely survive, eating one meager meal a day or one every other day, on about 250 rupees a year, or about 20 rupees a month. This is an exceedingly low estimate, with no allowance for clothes, household items, medicine, money to rent a room or repair one's own dwelling, and so on. Nevertheless, some thirty-two households of Kapileswar (about 5 percent) have earnings below this bare subsistence amount, and the people of these households are starving. Another one-third of the households with low-income earners subsist marginally. Insofar as they work, the people of these households earn enough to eat, but if they miss a day of work because of illness, they do not eat. The people of the remaining middle-income, well-to-do, and wealthy households live free from the threat of hunger in nondisaster years.

Table 7.6, a twenty-seven-point cumulative scale that includes nine points from each of the three scales of wealth (Tables 7.1, 7.4, and 7.5), provides an overall assessment of the wealth of each household of Kapileswar. One-fifth of the households are placed in what I term a privation category, which is characterized by three features: first, bare survival or below survival income; second, little or no additional wealth; third, little or no land. The families in this category have no protection against loss of income due to unforeseen but frequent disasters. The households (over 60 percent) which are in the low category live under conditions that are only slightly better, while the remaining households in the upper three categories live comfortably.

Table 7.6. Cumulative Wealth Scale per Household (Combining Land, Other Wealth, and Income Scales)

Cumulative scale	3-6	7-14	15-20	21-24	25-27	
Classification	Privation	Low	Middle	Well-to-do	Wealthy	Totals
Households						
Native residents	101	306	82	4	5	498
Strangers	26	56	13	1	0	96
Entire village	127	362	95	5	5	594
Percentages	21.5	60.7	16.1	.8	.8	99.9

There are great variations by caste in the overall wealth of
households. Table 7.7 summarizes the contrasts between six castes
of Kapileswar that are representative of wealthy, middle, and poor
castes. The previous chapters have shown how these great disparities in land owned, wealth owned, and income earned have influenced directions of change in Kapileswar.

Debtors and Lenders in Kapileswar

In June 1971, I collected data on indebtedness of 159 households in Kapileswar which were or had been in debt between 1968
and 1971.[3] Of these households, 104 were in debt in 1971. The
villagers anticipated that other households would incur new indebtedness just before the November harvesting, when food becomes scarce.

In 1971 the impoverished Bauris had the highest number of
households in debt (46), but their loans were rather small, totaling only 2726 rupees, or an average of 59 rupees per household
in debt. Many additional Bauri householders wanted to take loans,
but they were refused as bad credit risks. Bauri agricultural householders with assured employment and income—owners, sharecroppers,
and agricultural servants—received loans that averaged twice the value
of loans given to householders with uncertain employment—agricultural wage laborers. Over 80 percent of the loans given to Bauris
were given by employers or professional moneylenders. The remaining loans came from friends and relatives. Over 60 percent
of the moneylenders were Mallias, and over 60 percent of the money
received came from Mallias. All but three of the ninety loans taken
by Bauris were secured without mortgages. Most employers and
all professional moneylenders charge a yearly 25 percent or more
interest, payable in paddy or in cash, on their loans. For short-
term loans, or loans without mortgages, interest rates are as high

---

[3] Some individuals were reluctant to discuss their debts because they were
embarrassed by them, while moneylenders did not wish to discuss the loans
they gave. Accordingly, the number of debtors and lenders is probably much
higher than my figures indicate.

Table 7.7. Comparison of the Wealth of Six Castes of Kapileswar

	Number of Households	Land Owned			Wealth Other Than Land			Average Annual Income			Cumulative Score	
		Total Acres per Caste	Average Acres per Household	Rank in Village	Total Rupees	Average Rupees per Household	Rank in Village	Total Rupees	Rupees per Household	Rank in Village	Average Village	Rank in Village
Native Castes												
Khuntia Brahman	13	103	7.92	1	415,000	31,923	1	18,800	1446	1	18.30	1
Mallia	225	308.2	1.37	9	876,440	3859	7	160,546	714	12	10.09	11
Oilpresser	17	91.3	5.37	2	357,250	21,015	2	18,600	1094	4	14.29	3
Bauri	100	3.5	.04	22	53,900	539	23	50,724	507	23	7.15	24
Strangers												
Brahman	28	81.3	2.9	4	53,900	1925	13	32,440	1159	3	10.57	10
Sea Fisherman	22	.2	.01	23	6600	300	25	11,638	529	21	6.73	26

as 37 percent. Significantly, over 60 percent of the ninety Bauri loans were exclusively for food.

The second largest group of debtors in Kapileswar is the Mallia caste, with nineteen households that took loans in 1971. Although Mallia households in debt numbered less than half of the Bauri debtors, their loans were much larger than those of the Bauris, totaling 7527, or 396 rupees per household in debt. The Mallias borrowed primarily from lenders of their own caste, most of whom were professional moneylenders. The Mallias, like the Bauris, claimed that the need for food was the primary reason for taking loans; and indeed food accounted for nearly half of the Mallia loans. Only four loans were for business, and only one for cultivation.

Of the remaining thirty-nine households of Kapileswar that took loans in 1971, twenty of them were from the agricultural castes of Cultivator, Herdsman, and Militia. About two-thirds of their loans were for agriculture; less than 20 percent were for food. Professional moneylenders provided two-thirds of the loans, while employers (landowners for sharecroppers) gave another 20 percent of the loans. The size of the loans for agricultural caste households averaged 104 rupees per Cultivating caste household in debt, 88 rupees for the Militia, and 90 rupees for the Herdsmen. About one-third of the money came from Mallia moneylenders.

The remaining nineteen households that took loans borrowed mainly from professional moneylenders. The scarcity of food was the most frequently cited reason (42 percent) why households took loans.

From 1968 through 1971, 141 households in Kapileswar lent money, and another 19 households and one government agency lent money to the residents of Kapileswar. In 1971 alone I have records of 91 households plus 10 households outside the village that lent money to the villagers.

The Mallias comprised 69 percent of the moneylending households (63 of 91) in 1971, and 63 percent of the moneylenders from 1968 through 1971. My data show that most lenders are small moneylenders whose total amount lent is under 500 rupees. From 1968 through 1971, over 50 percent of the moneylending households loaned less than 100 rupees. Although I do not have complete records of loans and lenders in Kapileswar, my data clearly indicate that moneylending is not confined to large lenders and wealthy households but is widely practiced by many castes and households, including low-income ones.

Women play an important role as moneylenders in Kapileswar, where they give small loans at high interest rates. In some Indian villages, moneylending by women is not considered acceptable (Epstein 1959:234-51). In contrast, the men and women of Kapileswar consider female moneylenders not only acceptable, but indispensable. Women who need loans are reluctant to approach a man; if they must deal with a male moneylender, they do it through his wife or some other woman in his household. But they prefer to borrow from women. Men often are embarrassed to borrow money, fearing that their prestige in the village will be lowered. Rather than borrow directly, they send their wives to women moneylenders. The men rationalize sending their wives to borrow money by saying that, in money matters, women do not have to worry about their prestige as men do.

Between 1968 and 1971, thirty-four women from four castes earned income as moneylenders. They were equally divided between widows and wives with living husbands.

Twenty-two of the thirty-four women moneylenders each lent a total of less than 100 rupees. Of the remaining twelve women who lent over 100 rupees, four headed their own households, while eight were in households run by males. Although many villagers said that some women lent large sums, from 1000 to 3000 rupees a year, my records of particular loans given from 1968 to 1971 do not show amounts of this size. Two women shopkeepers were among the moneylenders.

Land Transfers in Kapileswar

Between 1950 and 1971, 83 households of Kapileswar bought more land than they sold, while 101 households lost more land than they gained. The remaining 410 households showed no gain or loss in landholdings. The villagers bought 84.7 acres of cultivable paddy land and sold 98.15 acres, for a net loss of 13.45 acres. The villagers also sold slightly more house plots and dry land than they bought, for a net loss of .91 acres. Land sales thus indicated that the building of the New Capital has not led to a spectacular improvement in the wealth of the village as a whole.

The only castes that have gained more paddy land than they sold are the Misra Brahmans (gain of .5 acre) and the business castes of Oilpresser (gain of 2.76 acres), Betel Seller (gain of 6.0 acres), and Confectioner (gain of 9.44 acres). The Mallias lost 3.64 acres. The greatest loss was among the Goldsmiths, where none of the eleven households gained land, but six households lost a total of 7.1 acres. The virtually landless Bauris lost a large fraction of what little land they had, 3.1 acres. The Sweepers also lost 3 acres.

There are a number of traditionally well-to-do households that are retaining their lands, and also a number of households, from many castes, that are on the economic ascent. Together, these households comprise about 20 percent of the village. The gains of these successful households are overridden by the larger numbers of households in their castes that are on the economic decline, and are selling their lands not only to other villagers but to outsiders.

The sale of paddy lands does not necessarily mean that a household is experiencing economic difficulties. True, the villagers express strong sentiments against selling paddy lands, which provide a household's food. But with the growth of a new city, it might be expected that some households would sell lands in order to have the capital to finance new business or manufacturing enterprises. My records show that since 1950 the residents of Kapileswar have sold 187 parcels of land (paddy lands plus dry lands), but only eighteen of these land sales were for business investments or for profit from increasing land prices. The most frequent reason that parcels were sold was to pay for rituals. Sixty-one parcels (33 percent of the sales) financed marriage and funeral ceremonies. The second most frequent reason (forty-one sales) was to buy food, while the third most frequent reason (twenty-four parcels) was to pay back loans that were due. Ten parcels were sold to pay for medicine, and twelve were sold to pay for litigations. In summary, the overwhelming number of land sales did not bring in capital that could be used for business or economic growth, but simply staved off economic disaster or enabled families to perform their social obligations at ritual occasions.

Portraits of Starvation and Affluence

The numerical data of this chapter give some idea of the magnitude of poverty and the range of wealth in Kapileswar. But this account would not be complete without presenting glimpses of what poverty as well as affluence is like for the individuals who experience it. The following reports are taken from interviews and full-length autobiographies that I collected from Kapileswar villagers, and from events that I witnessed.

A Bauri's View of Starvation

Muli sits on the veranda of his windowless mud and thatch hut. He is a forty-two-year-old Bauri, slender, ravaged by a lung disease, and too ill to work. He is supported by his wife, who left at dawn to transplant paddy in the fields of an Oilpresser. It is the rainy season, and the dirt road outside Muli's house has become an impassable swamp of mud. Although it is midday, Muli has not eaten since the previous night, for there is no food in his house. Despite his hardships, Muli says that he has seen worse times, and he describes one of them to me.

Before the harvest came in November, rice became very scarce; prices rose, and no one would lend us rice. We could not find any work, so we had no money to buy food. In order to survive, we dug up roots and stole yams from the fields of wealthy landowners. Even then, we were hungry. We ate one meal a day, or none. Sometimes we ate one meal every other day.

Right at harvest time, my infant son developed boils. They soon spread to my body, all over except my face. It was severe and painful. I could not walk because of the pain, so I could not harvest paddy, at the one time we could expect to have steady work. My wife also developed boils and could not work. My father, mother, and brother went to cut paddy. Mother resented that my wife and I were earning nothing, and she refused to give us any food. But my sister stole food from the kitchen and fed us. We sat at home, in agony, covered with boils. Whenever my mother found us eating, she scolded us and told us to leave, "Two people will sit in the house and eat," she said, "and there is their son, who requires two to three coins worth of sugar each day! So we feed three people every day from our earnings. Why aren't you looking after your own stomachs? We cannot feed you any more!"

Each night my wife cried under my feet. And we both prayed to God to cure us.

One morning I hobbled to the hospital, hoping to get some help from a doctor I knew. But he had been transferred; another doctor was there whom I did not know. I was a man of small caste, an untouchable, so I despaired. How could I talk to an important man like that? I turned away and returned home.

I was such a lucky man that my boils, instead of going away, got bigger day by day, and so did those of my wife. Meanwhile, my mother scolded us more and more.

My wife could no longer stand the scolding. One morning she borrowed some berries from a neighbor and sold them in the village. Even though she was in terrible pain, she worked; I couldn't do that. So I stayed home and took care of our infant son. I borrowed some sugar on credit from a high-caste shopkeeper. I mixed the sugar with water and fed it to my son two to three times that day. When my wife returned she nursed him. With the money she earned I went to the market and bought rice, sulphur, and cocoanut oil. It was very painful for me to walk. My wife boiled the sulphur and oil together, spread the hot paste on our boils, and soon they burst, and pus drained out. Throughout the day, up to that time late at night, we had not eaten anything. Now we ate. That night, for the first time in weeks, we were able to sleep without horrible pain, and with our bellies full.

But the boils returned. We survived like this for one month, with my wife working while I took care of our child, feeding him sugar water until his mother returned late at night and nursed him. Sometimes during that month we were able to eat even twice a day. My mother saw this and was jealous. She picked quarrels with my wife, screaming, "Who took my fuel, my rice, my vegetables? You did!"

Finally, my wife could stand this no longer, and answered harshly, "Who is taking your property? Whose pubic hair cares for your property?" This was a grave insult to give to one's respected superior, so my mother hit her, and they fought, screaming curses at each other, "You daughter of a whore! You cholera-eaten corpse! Leprosy will eat away your fingers!"

The women of the ward ran in and pulled them apart. The following day my wife and I separated from my father's household.

Anxieties over Food in a Bauri Women's Quarrel

Among the Bauris, anxieties over food are ever-present, and they surface to conscious expression on the slightest provocation. On the morning of March 23, 1971, while observing behavior in a Bauri ward of Kapileswar, I witnessed a brief but explosive quarrel between two Bauri grandmothers that revealed their deep-seated fears of starvation. The wage-earning males and females of the ward had already departed for their work sites, leaving behind small children under the supervision of their grandmothers. Several boys about six to seven years of age were playing near a house when suddenly one of them pushed his hand in a hole and it became stuck. The child cried out in alarm; women and older chil-

Plate 23.   While his mother works in the fields, a Bauri infant is cared for by his elder brother and his grandmother.

dren, fearing he might be bitten by a poisonous snake, ran over to help him, but by the time they reached him he had pulled his hand free.

Osa, the boy's grandmother, who was bent over with swollen joints, accused another boy of causing her grandson to put his hand in the hole. Koki, the accused boy's grandmother angrily defended her grandson,

"How can I do anything about it? The children are playing and they know who is responsible. My grandson did not do this. Is he so mischievous that he has to listen to such bad language from you? It's your child who is bad, no one else. Why don't you look after him?

Why don't you quit sitting on your ass and look after your own grandson?"

Osa replied,

> "If my grandson is poisoned by a snake, who is responsible then? I am the custodian; my son and daughter-in-law are working and giving me food to care for their child. I am a poor woman. If the child is hurt, my son may throw me out. My son feeds me. You may not like your grandchildren because your own son does not give food to you. That's why you don't look after your grandchild."

Koki waved her long bony arms wildly, and her loose waist-length hair flew back and forth as she screamed,

> "Who told you that I do not get food from my son? My son is good, he gives me food. But sometimes your son beats you. My son never beats me. I am in a better position than you!"

Osa laughed and mocked her,

> "Oh, your grandson will never praise you when he grows up because, due to your negligence, he is very bad. Rather, he will bite you! If your grandchild lives, do you think he will put you on a throne when he grows up? Never. Rather, he will throw you out, like Api!"

Osa pointed towards the roofless collapsed hut of Api, the beggar, a 70-year-old widow who was abandoned by her son.
Koki screamed,

> "I have three sons. When they are all grown up we will be more wealthy than you. They will bring home more money because they are big and strong. All your sons are separated. Only one son stays in your house, and only he and his wife are earners. This is a small amount. Sometimes you are starving. But we never starve. Your son does not like you. Sometimes he does not give you food. Though your son and his wife are earning, sometimes they don't give anything to you, so why are you praising them?"

In reply, Osa sat down on a house veranda, and bowing back and forth, chanted insults,

> "Your sons are thieves, like your first son, who has gone to jail three or four times. That is why he does not stay in the village. He works in Cuttack city, in a food stall, cleaning the plates, the nastiest

Plate 24.   A seven-year-old Bauri girl feeds her younger brother while their mother is working in the fields.

job, because the people here don't like him, and because the police are after him. You boast about being rich and having food every day, but actually you do not get food every day. Who gives you food? Your son is in Cuttack and gives you nothing. Your husband is old and cannot earn much. Your small sons work for a Herdsman and don't give you anything. You make an empty boast about how many children you have, but they are useless!"

Suddenly Osa stood up and walked away, and the quarrel abruptly ended, five minutes after it had started.

Why should a harmless boy's accident prompt such a vituperative exchange between the two grandmothers? The fate of the child appeared less important in the argument than what might happen to the grandmothers if the child had been hurt. The argument quickly passed from consideration of the child to the fears of the two old women: whether or not they received food from their sons; and whether or not their sons might beat them and throw them out to starve. In light of the harsh realities of Bauri economic life, these fears are not unrealistic.

A Mallia's Recollections of Childhood Starvation

Kedar, a 57-year-old leader with chiseled features and a medium build, sits on a slippery stone ledge with his feet dangling in the water of the Kapileswar temple tank. He is clad only in the briefest of orange cloths around his waist. A cooling water-soaked cloth rests on his head. In his right hand he holds a six-foot bamboo fishing pole. Kedar shows me the hook at the end of the line to which he has affixed his special bait. The fish he catches will be used to supplement his family's midday meal. As we sit waiting for the fish to bite, he begins to narrate his life history to me.

Unlike most leaders, Kedar did not come from a well-to-do family. Kedar, who works as a temple priest and a sharecropper, and who has failed in two business ventures, is one of many Mallias who are poor but not starving. For Kedar, however, his present economic condition is a vast improvement over his childhood days of starvation. Many poor Mallias on occasion have experienced privations like those described by Kedar:

> I was the fifth of six sons of a family of temple priests. Our ancestral home was just a few steps from our village temple, where my father performed the hereditary rituals of our caste, and served pilgrims who visited our temple. Since my father was landless and earned very little from the pilgrims who visited our village temple, he also worked as a pilgrim guide for a priest of a larger and wealthier temple in the nearby town.
>
> When I was nine years old, my father died. Soon after, my three elder brothers separated from the family. My mother's brother adopted my fourth brother, while I and my younger brother remained with my mother.
>
> We were alone and very helpless. We had no food to eat, and my elder brothers never helped us. My mother was a proud woman who told us never to go to them for meals. I was in the fourth grade, attending the primary school in the next village. I often went to school hungry. When I returned there was no food in the house. I had already skipped one grade, but I was still the best student in my class. Nevertheless, I quit school.

One day my teacher came to my house and asked me why I did not show up for school. I told him, "I am not eating, so how can I go to school and study?"

He invited me to stay in his house, take meals there, and continue my education. I did this for two months, but then stopped because I wanted to help my mother. Also, I did not want to accept charity. I tried to find work, but I was only nine years old. There was no work for me.

At that time my mother was not working. From time to time my father's sister, who had married into the wealthiest family of our caste, would steal leftover rice and curry from their meals, and sometimes snacks like puffed rice. She brought these to us even though her family disapproved and tried to prevent her. Without this food we would not have lived.

We ate perhaps once every two or three days. We never knew when we might receive food, or not. We lived like this for two years.

Once, when I was eleven, we went for several days and nights without eating. We had nothing but water. I was so weak that I could hardly walk or move. One morning I looked desperately around the house for something to sell. I found a brass pot for eye make-up in a cane box. I took the pot to a Confectioner caste man and exchanged if for about one kilogram of puffed rice. I took it home and asked Mother to bring some water to take with the puffed rice.

My mother became furious, and she scolded me, "Why did you beg to get this food? Throw it away."

I told her that I had not begged, but sold a pot for it. She accepted my statement, so we all ate. Mother took a very small amount. We lay down for a nap, but I could not sleep. I thought, "Now we had a snack, but how can we get a real meal of boiled rice?" I stood up and looked through the house until I found something else worth selling, an old palm leaf manuscript on history. I sold it to a wealthy man of my caste for one-half of a rupee. With the money I bought rice, lentils, firewood, oil, mustard seeds, spices, salt, and chili peppers. When I took these home, my mother again scolded me for begging. After I explained that I had sold our precious old palm leaf manuscript, she took a portion of the food and cooked it. My brother and I ate almost all of it; Mother took what was left, along with some thick rice water. We had survived another day.

In the afternoon I went back to the wealthy man's house, where I took a nap on his big wooden bed. I often took my afternoon naps in that house. After some time one of the servants of the household awakened me and said, "The master is coming to take his nap, so you have to move."

I replied, "I do not have the strength, I am too weak. I can't move, so let your master sleep somewhere else."

The servant became angry at my impertinent remarks, and told his master what I had said. The master strode into the room. I just lay there, looking up, too weak to move. I was so thin that my bones showed. The master was a kind-hearted man. He looked me over carefully. When he saw my shrunken appearance, he exclaimed, "Why didn't you tell me that you were starving? Today you were able to purchase rice, but what will you do tomorrow?"

I replied, "We will see what God will provide."

When he heard this, the wealthy man handed me a sickle and sent me to work cutting paddy in his fields. So now I had a job.

Throughout that harvest, I worked every day in his fields. It was very hard for an eleven-year-old. The work was so difficult that I often cried a lot from the pain. I frequently cut my hands. But what could I do? If I did not work, my mother, brother, and I would not eat. So I continued despite the pain, working with bleeding, raw hands. I earned one bundle of paddy for every twelve that I cut. We lived on the paddy I took home.

When the harvest was over I found that I had saved about twenty-five kilograms of paddy. That gave me the idea to set up a source of income for my mother. I went to the priest who had employed my father as a temple guide. When he heard my plan, he gave me five rupees, which I used to buy another twenty-five kilograms of paddy. We borrowed a husking pedal from my father's sister's daughter. My mother earned one-quarter of one rupee a day from boiling rice and pounding it with the pedal to remove the husk. Her income from this was just enough to feed the three of us, with nothing left over.

Crises of an Affluent Oilpresser

The crises of the poor center on starvation; those of the wealthy focus on costly litigations and labor disputes. Jogi, forty-five years old, fat and balding, complains that the Bauri wage laborers who cultivate his twenty-five acres of paddy land are greedy: "They want to be paid one bundle of paddy for every ten they cut instead of their proper wage—one for twelve." He pauses to daub lime paste on a shiny green betel leaf which rests on a polished red stone slab. He sprinkles the leaf with slivers of areca nut, spices, and tobacco, deftly folds the leaf into a cone, and pops it into his mouth. Each day he chews over 100 of these betel concoctions, spending twice as much for his habit as the households of his workers spend each day for food.

Jogi sits near me on a blue and white cushioned mat in a room on the second floor of his ten-room stone house. Above him an electric fan turns slowly; at his side a large table radio blares film songs. While Jogi's household is one of ninety-two in the village that have electricity, and one of twenty-five that have running water, few if any of the other households have a profusion of luxury items such as Jogi's household: five wrist watches, three bicycles, two overhead fans, a large radio, a bottled-gas stove, a toaster, a refrigerator, a shower, and a latrine with a flush toilet under construction.

The room that Jogi sits in is lined with metal trunks which contain books. Although he has only a seventh-grade education, Jogi is an avid reader of history and literature, and his library, which contains hundreds of books in the Oriya and Bengali languages, is the largest in the village. On the lime-plastered walls of Jogi's room are faded family photographs as well as lithographs of popular Hindu deities. Many loin cloths, shoulder cloths, and vests hang from wires strung across the room. One doorway opens onto a porch with elaborate ornamental stone railings. Another doorway leads to a dark narrow room, a portion of which is set aside for the household shrine. High, narrow, winding stone steps descend to a large front room on the first floor which is used for entertaining visitors. A narrow corridor leads from the front room past storerooms stacked with bags of rice to the kitchen area where Jogi's wife is preparing the midday meal: rice, lentils, two vegetable curries, and fish curry. This is typical fare for Jogi's household, in which expensive items like meat or fish are served nearly every day.

I ask Jogi why he hires inefficient wage laborers instead of more highly skilled sharecroppers, who produce higher yields and better profits. He shakes his head petulantly and says,

> "I used to hire sharecroppers. But two years after the great fire in Kapileswar (1959) my Bauri sharecroppers told me that they would no longer give me my owner's traditional one-half share, but only one-fourth. They got their idea from a new law which said that they only had to give their masters one-fourth, and that they couldn't be thrown off the land if they had worked it for several years. Nevertheless, I evicted them, and in revenge they took the entire crop for themselves. My lands were three miles from the village, so I could not watch and stop them. The next year, they forcibly occupied my lands, cultivated them, and again took the entire crop for themselves. I took them to court to get back my land. It took three years for the case to be decided, and during that period the Bauris retained control over the crops, which they harvested. But in 1962 the court ruled in my favor. The Bauri people could not read or write; they had no written proof that they had been the traditional sharecroppers of my lands. So the court

ordered them evicted, and I hired some wage laborers who are now
giving me trouble. If they don't accept the payment I give them, I'll
hire other workers to replace them next year."

Jogi's other sources of income helped him to weather the loss
of income from his crops. He is a moneylender, and in addition
runs a cloth shop in the New Capital market. Like many of the
wealthy households of Kapileswar, Jogi's household has become involved in several litigations. In 1946 Jogi's father started an inheritance dispute over property worth one quarter of a million rupees.
As of 1972 the case had dragged on for some twenty-six years,
costing Jogi upwards of 20,000 rupees. The case is now in the higher courts. When I asked him whether the case was worth the time
and money involved, Jogi shrugged, "We have won in the higher
courts, but of course the other side is appealing. Perhaps my grand-
children will benefit from the result."

Wealth, Opportunities, and Constraints

By village standards, the wealthy and well-to-do households of
Kapileswar, who are the primary recipients of benefits from the
New Capital, maintain high standards of living and are avid consum-
ers of new products and luxury items. Their wealth gives them much
greater flexibility than the poor in choosing new opportunities. The
New Capital has provided the wealthy with the opportunity to try
new occupations, products, and life-styles.

In contrast, the development of the New Capital has not been
good to the poor of Kapileswar. Despite twenty years in an urban
boom town environment, 60 percent of the households of Kapileswar remain poor, virtually landless, with uncertain incomes, and they
are unable to benefit significantly from the new opportunities that
the New Capital affords. Thus most of the loans that the villagers
take are simply for food or medicine and are not used for starting
businesses or furthering their children's education. The villagers
have sold more paddy lands than they have bought; only the three
business castes and one Brahman caste own more land in 1972 than
they did in 1950. The paddy lands of Kapileswar, even those that
in theory are inalienable temple trust lands, are gradually passing

into the hands of outsiders. Although incomes have increased, very few families have made the trasition from poor to middle-income or well-to-do status.

The economic constraints which prevent the poor from taking advantage of the New Capital include: first, an inequitable distribution of land, in which a small number of households own a large percentage of the land; second, an inequitable distribution of wealth other than land, in which only a small percentage of the households of the village have money for investments in businesses or their children's education; third, a large number of households with low earnings from occupations with uncertain employment that fluctuates in a shrinking job market; fourth, high interest rates on loans, which undermine a household's ability to accumulate wealth.

Faced with such liabilities, it is not surprising that many households become locked into a descending spiral—from which they cannot escape—which pulls them below the survival level. Typically this occurs when a combination of natural disasters such as drought and illness hit at the same time. Once ill and unable to work, weakened by hunger, malnutrition, and disease, the poor of Kapileswar consider themselves fortunate if they barely survive.

CHAPTER EIGHT

The Rise
of Formal Education
in Kapileswar

The Growth of the Kapileswar School

In 1914 the villagers of Kapileswar founded a *chatasala* 'informal school', which was conducted outdoors, and they hired a teacher, who instructed pupils in arithmetic and literature. The British government of Orissa paid the teacher four rupees per month, while the parents of his pupils supplied his meals. This school was the basic institution for educating higher-caste male children; those who were untouchables or from lower castes were not permitted to attend, nor were girls. The pupils were not divided into classes; rather, they attended until they lost interest or acquired basic reading and writing skills. If they were among the few who desired further education, they attended other schools in the Old Town and neighboring villages. The most highly educated villagers of Kapileswar had about a seventh-grade education.

In 1938 a Khuntia Brahman and several Mallias collected and donated funds to build a permanent stone schoolhouse, staffing it with teachers for a nursery class and the first three grades. The villagers built the school at the edge of a Mallia ward. Once the school was in operation, the government supplied teachers. Like the previous informal school, only high-caste and middle-caste male children attended, and most of them stopped when they had completed the third grade.

Prior to 1945 only one villager from Kapileswar—a Khuntia Brahman—had attended high school in the Old Town. Aside from this high school, there were no secondary schools in the Bhubaneswar area. The closest college was twenty miles away in Cuttack city, and the villagers from Kapileswar did not attend it.

In 1949 a Mallia youth became the first villager to enroll in a college. Forced to move to Puri, since Bhubaneswar still had no colleges at that time, he had completed one year when his father died. The young man had to return to the village to support his father's household. He became a high school teacher in the Old Town and subsequently a leader of the Mallias.

In 1954 the Mallias financed the building of new schoolrooms for grades four and five. By 1964 the school had expanded up to the seventh grade, and by 1972, through the tenth grade. The Kapileswar school was scheduled to extend through the eleventh grade— the final year of high school—by 1973.

The growth of the Kapileswar school in the past two decades occurred as a response to a basic literacy campaign stimulated by both the federal and state governments of India. In an effort to bring education to the untouchables, who traditionally had been excluded from schools, the government required that untouchables be admitted to public schools and be supplied with free books, supplies, and tuition. In colleges and professional schools, such as medical schools, places were reserved for untouchables, tribals, and women.

The construction of the New Capital near the village accelerated the school program for the villagers by creating new needs for education. Suddenly an education through secondary school and college became the passport to immediate placement in a growing bureaucracy of state and municipal governments. The New Capital not only fostered these needs, but provided the means to realize them. In the 1950s and 1960s, a host of colleges, universities, and training programs were established in the New Capital, including a coeducational undergraduate college, an agricultural university, a women's college, and a training program for workers involved in village agricultural development. In addition, Utkal University, the state university of Orissa, which offers graduate studies through the Ph.D., was moved from Cuttack to a new campus in the New Capital of Bhubaneswar.

In this environment of rising educational expectations, Kapileswar has shown a great increase over the past two decades in the number and percentage of villagers who have become literate.

Table 8.1.   Literate and Illiterate Villagers in 1971

Age:	Male 6-29	30 and up	Female 6-29	30 and up	Totals Male	Female	Totals
Native Residents							
High-Caste							
Literate	272	167	165	42	439	207	646
Illiterate	31	86	70	228	117	298	415
Middle-Caste							
Literate	93	50	45	11	143	56	199
Illiterate	7	38	31	79	45	110	155
Low-Caste							
Literate	45	24	14	2	69	16	85
Illiterate	7	23	21	44	30	65	95
Untouchable-Caste							
Literate	53	52	14	2	105	16	121
Illiterate	56	58	101	119	114	220	334
Strangers							
High-Caste							
Literate	38	25	29	7	63	36	99
Illiterate	3	2	4	11	5	15	20
Middle-Caste							
Literate	22	18	16	6	40	22	62
Illiterate	5	4	7	10	9	17	26
Low-Caste							
Literate	26	13	5	1	39	6	45
Illiterate	10	7	22	20	17	42	59
Untouchable-Caste							
Literate	1	0	0	0	1	0	1
Illiterate	0	1	1	2	1	3	4

This becomes evident by comparing the number and percentage of literate villagers who are above the age of thirty with those who are below that age. As Table 8.1 shows, literacy varies not only by age, but also by caste and sex. The highest ratio of literates to illiterates is found among high-caste males under the age of thirty, while the lowest ratio is found among untouchable females over the age of thirty. Thus the data on literacy in Kapileswar replicates what has already been observed in occupational selection and economic changes: the benefits from the New Capital are concentrated in the hands of traditionally wealthy and upper-caste households.

Between 1954 and 1962 the number of school children from Kapileswar in the first to fifth grades more than doubled—from 98 to 226. An additional twelve children, all of them untouchable Bauris from Kapileswar, attended an informal school in another village. By 1971 the enrollment in the Kapileswar school was 267, with another 47 children attending an informal school. Since 1962 the enrollment of the Kapileswar school has included students from neighboring villages.

Although the number of students increased, the dropout rate for each class as it progressed from grades one through five remained the same—about one-third. Many of the dropouts failed; others had parents who did not care whether or not their children attended school. Frequently these children themselves chose when to terminate their education.

In 1962 ninety-three Kapileswar villagers had had some high school or college education. Nearly 30 percent of these people were strangers, although strangers comprised less than 10 percent of the village population. These strangers were high-caste Brahmans or Scribes from civil service households.

By 1971 the number of residents who had attended high school or college had increased to 236 individuals. Strangers still comprise a high percentage of these students, including nearly half of those who attended college (see Table 8.2).

Table 8.2.   Residents of Kapileswar Who Are in or Have Completed High School or College in 1971

	High School		College		Totals		
	M	F	M	F	M	F	Totals
Natives	134	8	25	1	159	9	168
Strangers	31	14	21	2	52	16	68
Subtotals	165	22	46	3	211	25	236
Totals	187		49		236		

Education of Females

It is no accident that the education of females in Kapileswar lags far behind that of males, but the reasons for this great difference vary by caste.   Those of high and middle caste are concerned with the social and moral effects of education on their women. Thus, in 1962 higher-caste villagers were willing to give their daughters no more than five years of elementary schooling. Women marry soon after they reach puberty, and since they become wives and mothers, further education was considered unnecessary for them. Furthermore, household elders, both male and female, believed that the education of a girl would make her less easy to control by her in-laws or potential in-laws, in whose house she might reside after marriage. Finally, in 1962 any girl who continued her education beyond the fifth grade had to attend school in Old Town Bhubaneswar.

High school education, then, not only delayed a girl's marriage and made her a threat to in-laws, but also created the situation of a post-puberty girl traveling alone outside of the village. Middle- and high-caste villagers viewed this as immoral, or very close to it. Consequently, girls attending high school in the 1960s had to weather a great deal of gossip from disapproving village elders. An instance of this occurred in 1960 when one Mallia and two Brahman households of Kapileswar became the first to enroll their girls in the Old Town high school. (The Brahman girls are not included in my 1962 census since they married outside of the village.) The villagers bitterly criticized the parents of these girls for sending them to high school and even accused one of the Brahman girls of behaving improperly—according to village standards—because of the corrupting influence of education on women. All three girls were pulled out of the high school; in 1963 no girl native to Kapileswar was permitted to attend high school, and only three girls (one Brahman and two Mallias) attended the sixth or seventh grades. In summary, the formal education of Kapileswar girls in 1963 was minimal, and public pressure within the village tended to perpetuate this situation.

Nevertheless, in 1962 prejudices against educating women beyond grade school were being challenged, particularly by high-caste youths with civil service jobs who refused to marry illiterate and poorly educated women. Mallia elders realized that their daughters had a better chance to marry high-prestige government clerks if the daughters themselves were given a better education. The main obstacle became not education as such, but the fact that the women had to travel outside of the village to go to school. The Mallia solution was to expand the village school, thus satisfying the demands of traditional moralists as well as those of educated youths.

The figures of women's school enrollment in 1971 show a great increase over 1962. While the overall percentage of females attending school has not changed in the past decade, a higher percentage of females are now in the higher grades, as is shown in Table 8.3. Since enrollment in the upper classes now is limited by the size of the classrooms, a number of aspiring high school students from Kapileswar, including women, have been denied admission on the basis of their school records. These students are forced to enroll in the Old Town high schools. Faced with educating their women or hurting their prospects for marrying clerks, the high- and middle-caste villagers now allow their women to attend school outside the village. Despite gains, the education of high- and middle-caste females in Kapileswar lags behind that of males. More females than males who are of school age (ages 6-14) do not attend school. Moreover, parents do not allow women to marry men whose education is less than theirs. Consequently, several women have been forced to leave school by their parents, who feared that their daughters were reducing their eligibility for marriage by being too highly educated.

In summary, education for middle- and high-caste women has become a factor in marriage negotiations, but because of caste disapproval education has not become a means to enter the job market.

Table 8.3. The Percentage of Kapileswar Females per School Class in 1962 and 1971 (Formal School)

| | Grades | | | | | Total of all Grades | | |
	1-3	4-5	6-7	High School 8-11	College	Number of Females	% of Class	Total in Class (M and F)
1962	30.7	39.1	7.0	0	0	69	(29.9)	231
1971	37.1	29.9	30.8	13.9	20.0	121	(29.5)	411

In 1972 a high-caste wage-earning woman was viewed as a threat to potential in-laws, as well as to caste and family prestige. This accounts for the fact that no woman from Kapileswar has used her education to secure a wage-earning job.

The pressures against educating low-caste and untouchable women are no less intense, but for different reasons. Faced with the threat of scarce food, castes such as the Bauris need every available wage earner. While mothers and fathers work in the fields or on the roads, their school-age daughters care for younger brothers and sisters. When they reach the ages of 12 to 14, the daughters themselves become wage laborers, leaving the childrearing duties to younger sisters or grandparents who are too ill or weak to work as wage laborers.

The low and untouchable castes see no economic advantage to educating their daughters. The men they marry are poorly educated, and education does not improve a woman's prospects for marriage. In households where food and wage earnings are daily uncertainties, and where no males have yet been able to use education to find higher-paying jobs, educating women is not even considered. Among 100 Bauri households, three females attended an informal school for a few months and at best they are barely literate.

The Education of High- and Middle-Caste Males

In 1962 education beyond the fifth grade was limited almost exclusively to high- and middle-caste males. Most of them were from the high castes. The Brahmans alone, who comprised less than 10 percent of the village's population, accounted for one-third of these students. The Mallias constituted 38 percent of these students, but this also closely approximated the population percentage of Mallias in the village. In this respect, the Mallias resembled the middle castes of Kapileswar, who comprised 19 percent of the population and 21 percent of the post-fifth-grade students.

By 1962 the aspirations of high school education for males had filtered down to the middle castes. In the 1960s the sudden appearance of college students in Kapileswar resulted from the construction of a college in the New Capital. This college especially encouraged higher education in the 1960s because it enabled the students from Kapileswar to remain at home with their families and friends, which they preferred to do. Most important, it enabled the students to hold government jobs while attending the night college; in 1962 four out of six Mallia college students did this.

Because many middle- and high-caste villagers viewed education solely as a means to secure a government clerk's job, they were impatient with those aspects of the primary and secondary schools, such as the teaching of gardening and simple crafts, which did not directly prepare students to pass the government service examinations and which, as manual tasks, were considered demeaning and low-caste activities.

Parents also criticized new ideas which they did not comprehend. For example, one parent complained that the school taught his child that the world was moving. The parent considered this idea both useless and unreasonable since it contradicted the evidence of his senses— he reasoned that if the world were really moving, he should see the well on his village street moving.

Parents were especially critical of overcrowding in the schools and the inability of teachers to give individual attention to the students. As a result, many parents hired private tutors; or, if they had sufficient education, tutored their own children to give them an advantage in school competition. The poorly paid schoolteachers frequently moonlighted as private tutors, thus encouraging poor teaching in school while increasing the demand for private tutoring. The institution of tutoring is widespread throughout India and is widely criticized for the reasons just stated.

In 1971 the number of middle- and upper-caste high school students in Kapileswar increased, but the number of college students decreased (see Table 8.4). The fact that the decline in the number of college students occurred during a period when government jobs became unavailable is no accident; it is the direct result of a changing job market. Since a college degree no longer guarantees a government job, many villagers are seeking other forms of education or training which will prepare them for other kinds of occupations.

Table 8.4.   Highest Grade Attended in 1971 by
Villagers of Kapileswar

	High	Middle	Low	Untouchable	Total
Native residents					
Grades 6-7	82	23	13	8	126
High school	86	19	9	5	119
High school pass	22	2	1	0	25
College	12	4	1	0	17
College pass	8	4	0	0	12
Total native residents	210	52	24	13	299
Strangers					
Grades 6-7	10	7	3	0	20
High school	13	14	2	0	29
High school pass	14	4	0	0	18
College	9	3	1	0	13
College pass	8	2	0	0	10
Total strangers	54	30	6	0	90
Total village					
Grades 6-7	92	30	16	8	146
High school	99	33	11	5	148
High school pass	36	6	1	0	43
College	21	7	2	0	30
College pass	16	6	0	0	22
Total villagers	264	82	30	13	389
Percentage	67.9	21.1	7.7	3.3	100.0

The Education of the Lower- and Untouchable-Caste Males

In 1962 the untouchable castes comprised 20 percent of the village population, but none of the untouchables had more than a fifth-grade education. The low castes, with 10 percent of the village population, contributed only 2 percent of the Kapileswar students who studied beyond the fifth grade. There was one Barber who completed seven years of school and now holds a Class IV government job. Aside from him, the Potters were the only low caste which showed any interest in education beyond the fifth grade. Two children from this caste were in high school, hoping to become government clerks. Their families sold land to finance their education; other Potter caste families expressed a willingness to make economic sacrifices in order to push their children through high school. Eleven out of twelve children of school age in this caste were in school. The parents of all children in the fourth grade, or higher, hired additional private tutors for their children.

In 1962 the yearly expenses for each student increased with each succeeding class, from 40 rupees in the first grade to 150 rupees in the fifth. The expenses included ink, pens, paper, slate, and carrying bag, as well as books and clothes. The major expense then and now is clothing, since the school requires that all girls must wear dresses, while all boys must wear shorts and shirts. The untouchable castes of Kapileswar are supposed, in theory, to receive books and supplies at government expense, but clothing is not subsidized; moreover, these castes do not always get their subsidies. All other castes have to bear full expenses. In 1962, for example, a Potter family with a son in high school spent almost one-third of their annual income, 326 rupees, on education. Nearly half of the expense consisted of fees for private tutoring. Since so many children in Kapileswar use tutors, these fees might be considered part of normal school expenses. For the Potter's family just mentioned, the private tutor's fees totaled 144 rupees. The remaining 182 rupees were spent in approximately equal amounts on school tuition, books and supplies, clothes, and miscellaneous. The latter expense, which consisted of one-fourth of a rupee per day spent on films, food at the school, and tea, was considered a necessary school expense related to keeping up appearances as a student.

Such high expenses may have discouraged untouchables and low castes other than the Potters from giving education beyond the fifth grade to their children. Nevertheless, castes such as the Sweepers have enjoyed an increased income from the New Capital. It is clear, then, that in numerous cases a choice is made not to continue education even though the money is available. This choice is based on a short-term view in which a small but quick economic return on the educational investment is preferred to a larger but delayed return. The Sweepers explicitly state that they do not intend to give their children a high school education because they can get Class IV government jobs without additional schooling.

Nevertheless, the Sweepers have begun to encourage their boys to attend primary school. Between 1957 and 1962 the number of Sweeper children attending the Kapileswar school increased from two to seven. This represented a significant increase since there were only eleven Sweeper households in Kapileswar. By 1962 every Sweeper household with school-age children had at least one child in school. By 1971 thirteen Sweepers attended school, including one in the sixth grade and one in high school. Ten Sweeper children of school age did not attend school.

As early as 1960 the Sweepers were demanding equal treatment with other castes in the school and government-subsidized supplies, both of which were withheld from them by the Kapileswar headmaster. The Sweepers complained about this to higher educational authorities in Bhubaneswar—particularly the separation of their children into a corner of the classroom—and the Sweepers claim that their complaints forced the school to abandon this practice. The Sweepers still complain, however, that they do not get the supplies and books which are due them.

It is understandable that the Sweepers are the only untouchables to challenge the educational establishment of Kapileswar. There are only four powerless households of Washermen, while the Bauris are economically dependent on the Mallias and Brahmans. The Sweepers, who work for the municipal government, not only are wealthier and more independent than the other untouchable castes but, also, because of their jobs, they personally know government officials with whom they can register complaints. Furthermore, the Kapileswar school was built adjacent to the Sweepers' ward, at the edge of a Mallia ward. With the school right next door, the Sweepers have insisted that their children be admitted and given equal treatment with higher-caste students.

Prior to 1950 only one Bauri had been to a formal school. In 1962, 35 percent of the school-age Bauri children were attending school; but, by 1971, the percentage had dropped to 24 percent, all males (see Table 8.5). There were, however, three high school

Table 8.5.   Bauris in School

	Grades				Totals: School Age Children				
	Primary 1-5	Middle 6-7	High School 8-11	College	Number of Bauri Children	Number in School	% in School	Number Not in School	% Not in School
1950	0	0	0	0	—	0	0	—	0
1957	3	0	0	0	—	3		—	—
1962	23[a]	0	0	0	59	23	(35)	36	(65)
1971	23[b]	0	3	0	108	26	(24)	82	(74)

[a]Includes twelve children in an informal school.
[b]Includes thirteen children in an informal school.

students, a notable achievement considering the liabilities these children face. As previously mentioned, and as shown in Table 8.6, only three Bauri females have received any education.

The reasons for Bauri educational stagnation are more than economic. In 1962 the Bauri children knew that they were not welcome at the Kapileswar school. In order to reach it, they had to walk through hostile Mallia wards. Those Bauris who did attend were persecuted by the Mallia children, who threw stones and sand at them and provoked them into fights, while Mallia adults became angry at them when they fought back. Consequently, several Bauri laborers withdrew their children from the school. In 1962 only eleven of the twenty-three Bauri children remained at the Kapileswar school. The others attended a private but tuition-free school in the neighboring village of Santrapur. The school was run by a high-caste educator who encouraged the education of untouchables. In 1962 twelve Bauri children attended this school, but it ceased operation in the mid-1960s. In 1971 there was a new headmaster of the Kapileswar school who did not discriminate against the Bauris. Nevertheless, still fearing harassment from Mallias, only thirteen Bauri children were enrolled in that school, while thirteen attended another private school run by a Mallia who was free of discrimination.

Table 8.6.   Bauri Literacy in 1971

	Literate	Illiterate	Totals
Male	82 (43.0%)	106 (57.0%)	188 (100.0%)
Female	3 (1.5%)	198 (98.5%)	201 (100.0%)
Totals	85	304	389

Wealth, Education, and Opportunity

Before 1950 most of the villagers were illiterate. Between 1950 and 1962 there was a spectacular rise in the educational level of the village, leading to widespread literacy among the younger high-caste males. Some young untouchables and high-caste women became at least minimally literate.

Nevertheless, in 1962 the educational system perpetuated the caste and economic gap, since schooling beyond the fifth grade was limited almost exclusively to middle- and high-caste male pupils, who viewed education as a long-term investment for a high-paying and prestigious job with the government. Most of the low and untouchable castes had a short-term view of education which corresponded to their limited view of new occupational opportunities. Thus, as in economic change and occupational change, the hierarchy of aspiration in education matched the traditional hierarchy of caste and wealth.

In 1962 and 1971 the education of women also followed caste values and life-styles. Among the high castes, women were permitted to complete the fifth grade, but no more, until pressure from civil servants who wanted more highly educated wives forced reluctant parents to allow their daughters to continue in school. Nevertheless, high-caste men did not permit their women to work outside the house. The low castes and untouchables saw no opportunities for their women other than as full-time menial wage earners.

Thus in 1971 the caste, educational, and economic gap remained, despite the declining enrollment of high-caste college students and a slight increase in the number of untouchable and low-caste students who continued their education beyond the fifth grade. As occupational opportunities for the villagers changed, educational aspirations and needs within Kapileswar changed. Many lower-caste families saw greater opportunities in training their children to become bicycle mechanics rather than government clerks, and so their interest in formal education waned. Among the higher castes, educated youths were being encouraged to attend agricultural training programs, as villagers began to realize that government jobs were no longer available and, furthermore, that agriculture brought in a higher income than government service.

CHAPTER NINE

Conclusion

Reasons for the Directions of Change in Kapileswar

The three broad patterns of influence on life-styles which were singled out for study in this book are:

1. the effects of *caste* on life-styles;
2. the effects of *scarce resources* on life-styles; and
3. the effects of *new urban opportunities* on life-styles.

These effects were shown in each case as changes produced in the occupations, wealth, education, and religion of the villagers of Kapileswar, and thus offer a concrete foundation for the conclusions of this study.

Caste

People of different castes in Kapileswar are making widely varying choices in attempting to adapt their life-styles to changing economic and social circumstances caused especially by the construction of the New Capital at Bhubaneswar. The changes which the villagers make tend to follow caste lines. Despite two decades of urban growth, a large percentage of the people of Kapileswar remain desperately poor, with no new skills and little or no education. Very few of the poor have been able to move from poor to middle income status, and the gap between the poor and the wealthy is widening. Most of the poor come from the low and untouchable castes. The Bauris, who exemplify the plight of the low-status poor, seek unskilled construction jobs but, due to their fear of upper-caste reprisals, refuse to learn skilled masonry, are uninterested in sending their children to school, and, although they are now permitted to do so, remain reluctant to enter major shrines used by high-caste people. Although they avoid caste discrimination confrontations with high-caste villagers inside Kapileswar, the Bauris have not hesitated to become town oriented in their social activities.

A small percentage of the villagers, who were traditionally well off, are the major beneficiaries of the opportunities that the New Capital offers. Most of these persons have taken new remunerative jobs that are compatible with their caste status, or they have commercialized their traditional occupations. Some of them have taken advantage of new educational facilities, enabling them to qualify for jobs such as civil service. Their incomes have increased relatively faster than those of the poor. The castes that have benefited from the New Capital are the traditionally high castes and the middle-status business castes, both of which were traditionally well off. The Mallias and the Brahmans, who represent the traditionally privileged, prefer to acquire a higher education and government jobs. They avoid menial labor and, until recently, they avoided agricultural development. The wealthy business castes focus on business and are very successful; so they neglect higher education, government jobs, and cultivation.

In summary, differential changes in Kapileswar have occurred in ways that are closely related to traditional caste status, values, and wealth.

Scarce Resources

While caste values are important, they do not completely explain the choices that villagers make. Some people have turned to occupations and activities which are disapproved of though grudgingly allowed by the people of their caste. For example, some Mallias work at menial jobs, while many young Bauris have become musicians, a task previously considered beneath their station. Both of these choices clearly are influenced more by economic considerations than by caste values.

For the people of Kapileswar, especially the poor, scarcity profoundly influences the choices they make in order to survive. Consider the following major constraints that inhibit their economic development.

First, there is an inequitable land distribution. Fifty-eight percent of the households are landless, only 11 percent have enough land to be self-sufficient, while 1 percent of the households own nearly 30 percent of the land.

Second, there is a growing population and a scarcity of land. Even if the paddy lands of Kapileswar were to be equally distributed among each household, there would be only 1.4 acres per household, which, given present yields per acre, is not enough for each family to be self-sufficient.

Third, there is an inequitable distribution of wealth other than land. A few families have sufficient wealth to be able to invest it in businesses, or in the technical and higher education of their sons. Castes like the Bauris and the Sea Fishermen, as well as many families of Mallias, have no capital for investment.

Fourth, there are job scarcities. The Kapileswar temple, with its limited temple service positions, and the government, with its limited number of government jobs, have caused widespread occupational, social, and ritual changes among rapidly increasing Mallias and Brahmans. At the other end of the social and economic scale, the Bauri life-style has been greatly affected by limited numbers of available places for sharecroppers and even for agricultural cash wage laborers. There has been a slowdown in new construction projects in the city. Unskilled laborers find work no more than fifteen days a month. Although villagers are earning higher incomes than they did twenty years ago, for most of them their incomes have not been high enough to enable them to accumulate capital to any significant extent.

Fifth, scarcity also results from natural disasters which occur at least every other year, and these strike hardest at the people in the lower-income groups. Their mud and thatch houses are more easily damaged by cyclones and fires than are the stone houses of the wealthier villagers. The poor have no food reserves. Calamities and the destruction of crops lead to soaring food prices, to hunger, to widespread emigration from Kapileswar, to selling land and ornaments, and to increased indebtedness. Bauris and other poor villagers spend much of their income paying back, at the exorbitant interest rate of 37 percent, loans they were forced to take in order to eat. Scarcity prompts villagers to change their occupations, whether caste approved or not, it affects their ability to pay for an education, and it prompts family disputes over land and food.

The poor of Kapileswar are locked into a vicious circle of insufficient food (one meager meal every one or two days), lowered resistance to disease, and no money to pay for medicines. Medical care is free at hospitals and primary health centers, but medicines are not. The impoverished villagers of Kapileswar often neglect medical treatment, not because they are indifferent or do not know any better, but because they cannot afford even the cheapest medicine. When they are too ill to work and earn, they starve, and their condition rapidly deteriorates.

Some writers have argued that the Indian joint family, or the caste system, or Hindu spiritual values significantly impede Indians from modernizing. *In light of the crushing economic conditions that prevent the vast majority of impoverished villagers of Kapileswar from earning enough money to be able to eat regularly, let alone improve their economic lot, controversies over whether or not Hinduism, family structures, or caste behavior inhibit their modernization appear to be tragically beside the point.*

New Urban Opportunities

New opportunities also affect directions of change. The building of the New Capital at Bhubaneswar induced migrants to return from Calcutta, encouraged high-caste Brahmans and Mallias to abandon not only their economically unrewarding temple service but also their voluntary temple worship. New economic and social opportunities are responsible for the commercialization of the traditional tasks of Barbers and Washermen, the founding of numerous shops and businesses by nonbusiness castes, the aquisition of new skills such as automobile and bicycle repair, the abandonment of old village forms of leisure activity in favor of new ones in the New Capital, and the decline of old ritual performances and festivals in favor of new ones.

Furthermore, as economic and social opportunities change, villagers try to adapt to these new changes. Traditional businessmen selling in the New Capital find that if they are to survive they must change their old credit-giving procedures and their rigid exclusion of untouchables from their shops. Educated Mallias and Brahmans for whom government jobs might have been plentiful in the 1960s now find these jobs are all filled. Consequently, some of these young high-caste men are beginning to turn their attention to business and to learning improved methods of cultivation. Other castes are not able to adapt very well to these new changes. The previously well-to-do Goldsmiths of Kapileswar are out of work and selling off their lands for food. The untouchable Bauris, who found plentiful work as stone quarry and construction laborers in the 1960s, find themselves out of work with the slowdown of construction in the New Capital in the 1970s. The few Bauri children who are in the upper school grades are being educated for government jobs that do not exist.

Thus the opportunities of the 1960s have become the dead ends of the 1970s. The villagers of Kapileswar find themselves confronted once more with the crisis of adapting to a rapidly changing new world over which they have little control.

Reasons for the Decline of the Temple and the Rise of Popular Religion

The primary reason for the decline of the temple is obviously economic. Faced with a growing population on limited endowed lands, the temple did not have enough land to provide even minimum incomes for those who were qualified for temple employment.

The consequences for the temple were inevitable. Mallias and other temple workers sought occupations outside the temple. Those who remained at the temple fought over rights to serve pilgrims or prepare sacred food. Priests simplified or abandoned temple services when the cost of offerings exceeded the income they received from their miniscule parcels of temple land. The morale of temple servants deteriorated.

While the construction of the New Capital provided new occupations for the priests, thus reducing their dependence on the temple, the rise of the New Capital did not cause the decline of the temple, but rather hastened a deterioration that was already under way. As the New Capital expanded, some of its new residents patronized the Kapileswar temple, but not sufficiently to offset the economic decline of the temple.

In contrast, popular religion benefited from the growth of the urban center. Many patrons from the New Capital attended popular festivals such as fire-walking ceremonies and consulted shamanistic curers when they were beset with crises. These curers were less costly to support than were temple priests, since donations to priests had to be used to provide for both the priests and their temple. The Durga Festival celebrations were sponsored by businessmen in the Old Town and New Capital, without whose support the festival would not have expanded as rapidly and widely as it did.

A second reason for the decline of the temple was government interference in its management. Temples were frequently associated with caste factionalism and mismanagement by hereditary trustees, so government officials were understandably often unsympathetic to the plight of temples like Kapileswar, as the controversies over the ownership of the Kapileswar tank showed. In contrast, popular religious activities like fire-walking, the Three Lords Festival, and Durga Festival were not subject to the same official scrutiny and control from government officials.

Third, the temple traditionally was associated with elaborate ritualism and caste restrictions that were appropriate for village life but did not fit the ideology of independent India and the life-style of contemporary cities. The temple services epitomized rigid caste restrictions and separation. Moreover, the proper performance of temple rituals was complex and time consuming.

In contrast, the rituals of popular performances were more flexible, and the barriers of caste were loosened. In the Three Lords Festival, individuals of different castes sang together and shared offerings of food. At Durga Festival, multicaste neighborhoods that often were comprised of virtual strangers organized the festival and competed together as a group. Such intercaste festivals were not new to the Hindu tradition, but they received greater emphasis in urbanizing and modernizing settings. Mallia civil servants did not have time to perform the day-long temple rituals, but in the evenings they had time to sing at the Three Lords Festival.

Finally, faced with limited funds, the Kapileswar temple could not sponsor large spectacles, and spectator attendance declined. Patrons turned instead to popular festivals. Temple rituals did not have the immediacy and personal involvement of popular festivals. Pilgrims who visited the temple had rituals performed for them by hereditary priests. These rituals focused primarily on what Mandelbaum calls the long-term transcendental needs of clients (1964:5-20).

In contrast, popular rituals like the Three Lords Festival involved the direct participation of devotees, and usually focused on their immediate, practical needs or desires.

The Significance of Religious Changes in Kapileswar

What distinguishes Kapileswar from most Indian villages is that it is a temple community. As I have pointed out previously, for 500 years the Kapileswar temple has been the central institution of the village, controlling the economic, political, social, and ritual activities of the villagers, and providing them with a role as representatives of the temple that is an inseparable part of their identities. What happens to a community when a beloved institution that permeates the lives of its inhabitants begins to crumble?

My study shows that there is no evidence whatsoever of religious disintegration or secularization in Kapileswar, that is, the loss of a religious outlook or world view. My conclusions are in agreement with those of Singer (1972:140-44, 246, 385, 398-99). Singer found that religion did not disintegrate or secularize in the modernizing environment of Madras City in South India. New expressions of religion developed, which creatively utilized traditional elements. Moreover, the directions of change were not haphazard; they were adaptations to an urban rather than a rural environment. Specifically, religion shifted in emphasis from ritual to devotional forms. This is precisely what is happening in Kapileswar, where temple rituals are giving way to devotional rituals like the Three Lords Festival.

Second, despite rapid urbanization and the transition of the priests of Kapileswar to civil servants and businessmen, there is no evidence whatsoever that these modernizing priests suffered crises of faith, or viewed their traditional religious life-style as incompatible with the modernizing one of the town. Their crises, as well as those of other castes of the village, were economic and political, not religious.

Writers like Weber, Myrdal, and Levy have claimed that otherworldly religions like Hinduism, and life-styles like the Hindu lifestyle, are incompatible with modernization, and either will be destroyed by modernization or will hinder its development (Weber

1968:11, 122-23, 325-28; Myrdal 1968:1081, 1148, 1692; Levy 1966:613-15; 1972:3-10). My study, like that of Singer, questions any such hypothesis which claims that traditional world views are necessarily incompatible with rapidly changing and modernizing social environments, or that modernization, at least in its relatively early phases, necessarily produces secularization (Singer 1966:55-67; 1972:245-414). The contention that tradition and modernity are compatible in India is shared by other writers, like Mandelbaum and Lloyd and Susanne Rudolph (Mandelbaum 1972:638-54; Rudolph and Rudolph 1967:6).

Third, the religious changes that occurred in Kapileswar are in no way related to revitalization movements, in Wallace's use of the term (1956:264-81; 1966:157-66, 209-15; 1970:188-99). This is indicated by the fact that the changes that did occur reflected an extension of a previous life-style rather than taking on a wholly new life-style. For example, the Mallias and Brahmans of Kapileswar consider the role of a government clerk to have much in common with that of a temple priest, and the similarities make government service attractive to them. Both jobs are considered highly prestigious; both are embedded in a clear-cut hierarchy; both entail highly ritualized behaviors; and moreover, neither of them involve hard physical labor, which tends to be associated with low-prestige occupations. Furthermore, civil service is not a new occupation for Indians, even if it is new for the inhabitants of Kapileswar. For centuries, high-caste individuals have considered it an acceptable alternative to their hereditary caste occupations.

Finally, not only are the villagers not secularizing, they also are not converting to new faiths, either within or outside Hinduism. Their increased participation in devotional worship is not incompatible with temple traditions, but rather belongs to a long devotional tradition that has been an accepted part of Hinduism for centuries. The Mallias, including those who no longer serve the deity of the temple, remain proud of their caste and their hereditary position as representatives of the deity of Kapileswar. They believe in this deity as well as in his consort, Kali. They are proud to live within the boundaries of the sacred space of Bhubaneswar. They see themselves, often speak of themselves, as part of a religious tradition, a religious community. Each day the Mallias recite prayers and perform personal religious rituals. Clearly the basic symbols of their religious world view have not become questioned, even though they work in a modern environment. Their successful separation of personal religion from secular work is an example of a process of adaptation to modernization that Singer terms "compartmentalization" (1972:320-25).

Thus, despite changes in themselves, their temple, and their urbanizing village, the Mallias and the Brahmans of Kapileswar represent a community of religious specialists whose ritual, social, economic, and political lives once centered around a temple, and who have adapted with varying degrees of success, like the non-religious castes of the village, without anguish or loss of religious faith, to the diminishing influence of the temple.

Epilogue

For many years both the national and the state governments of India have been committed to improving the economic and social conditions of their people, and in many places they have achieved notable successes. The failures described in my study thus should not be interpreted to mean that urbanization and attempts at economic improvement elsewhere in India necessarily result in or are foredoomed to failure, but rather that failure can result from extreme conditions of poverty and scarce resources.

People in affluent cultures are accustomed to thinking optimistically that there are ready solutions to the problems that confront them.

The problem that the inhabitants of Kapileswar face is that, despite urbanization, only 20 percent of the population live without the fear of starving.

There is no foreseeable solution to their plight.

This book has provided a sobering glimpse of the pervasive effects of poverty and scarce resources in stifling modernization. Villagers like Kapileswar reveal a complex and elaborate social and ritual life, yet much of it is dominated by scarcity, natural calamities, and poverty. The problem faced by most of the villagers of Kapileswar was not that they resisted modernization or new urban influences; they were very receptive to changing their life-styles when they believed that it would benefit them. The tragedy of their life-style was that the villagers were never able to break away from a crushing environment of poverty that frustrated their every attempt to improve their economic condition.

Bibliography

BOOKS AND ARTICLES

Aiyer, V.G. Ramakrishna
    1946   *The Economy of a South Indian Temple*. Annamalainagar, India: Annamalai University Press.

Bailey, F.G.
    1957   *Caste and the Economic Frontier*. Manchester, England: Manchester University Press.

    1963   *Politics and Social Change: Orissa in 1959*. Berkeley: University of California Press.

Barber, Bernard
    1968   "Social Mobility in Hindu India." In *Social Mobility in the Caste System in India* (ed. James Silverberg), pp. 18-35. The Hague: Mouton.

Beals, Alan
    1961   "Cleavage and Internal Conflict: An Example from India." *The Journal of Conflict Resolution* 5:27-34.

Berreman, Gerald
    1965   "The Study of Caste Ranking in India." *Southwestern Journal of Anthropology* XXI (2):115-29.

Bhardwaj, Surinder Mohan
    1973   *Hindu Places of Pilgrimage in India*. Berkeley: University of California Press.

Bose, N.K. (ed.)
    1960   *Data on Caste in Orissa*. Calcutta: Anthropological Survey, India.

Care-Orissa
   1972   *Planning for Better Nutrition in Orissa.* Care-Orissa.

Census of India, 1961
   1966   *Orissa: District Census Handbook, Puri.* Cuttack: Orissa
           Government Press.

Census of India, 1971
   1971   *Orissa: Provisional Population Totals.* Cuttack: Orissa Govern-
           ment Press.

Cohn, Bernard
   1955   "The Changing Status of a Depressed Caste." In *Village India*
           (ed. McKim Marriott), pp. 53-77. Chicago: University of
           Chicago Press.

   1959   "Some Notes on Law and Change in North India." *Economic
           Development and Cultural Change* VII: 79-93.

   1971   *India: The Social Anthropology of a Civilization.* Englewood
           Cliffs, N.J.: Prentice-Hall.

Dalton, George (ed.)
   1967   *Tribal and Peasant Economics: Readings in Economic Anthro-
           pology.* Garden City, N.Y.: The Natural History Press.

Das, Kunjabehari
   1953   *Orissan Folklore.* Santiniketin, India: Santiniketin Press.

Derrett, J. Duncan M.
   1966   "The Reform of Hindu Religious Endowments." In *South
           Asian Politics and Religion* (ed. Donald Eugene Smith),
           pp. 311-36. Princeton: Princeton University Press.

DuBois, Cora
   1970   "Studies in an Indian Town." In *Women in the Field: Anthro-
           pological Experiences* (ed. Peggy Golde), pp. 221-36. Chicago:
           Aldine.

Dumont, Louis and David Pocock
   1957   *Contributions to Indian Sociology,* Vol. I. The Hague:
           Mouton & Co.

   1958   Vol. II. The Hague: Mouton & Co.

Epstein, T. Scarlett
    1959   "A Sociological Analysis of Witch Beliefs in a Mysore Village."
            Eastern Anthropologist 12 (4):234-51.

    1967   Reprinted in *Magic, Witchcraft, and Curing* (ed. John Middleton),
            pp. 135-54. Garden City, N.Y.: The Natural History Press.

Freeman, James
    1968   *Power and Leadership in a Changing Temple Village of India.*
            Ph.D. dissertation, Harvard University.

    1971   "Occupational Changes among Hindu Temple Servants."
            Indian Anthropologist 1:1-13.

    1974a   "Trial by Fire." *Natural History* 83 (Jan.):54-63.

    1974b   "Occupational Changes in an Urbanizing Hindu Temple Village."
            Man in India 54 (Jan.-March):1-20.

    1975   "Religious Change in a Hindu Pilgrimage Center." *Review of
            Religious Research* 16 (2):124-33.

    1976   "The Untouchable Tragedy." *The Geographical Magazine* London
            Vol. XLVIII No. 10, July, 611-617.

Government of India
    1961   *Census of India: 1961.* XII: Orissa, parts I-Ai, II-A, IX-A,
            and IX-B. Delhi: Manager of Publications, 1961.

Government of Orissa
    1969   *The Hindu Religious Endowments Act 1969.* Cuttack: Law
            Department, Government of Orissa.

    1972   *Report on the Sample Survey for Estimation of Loss in Yield
            Rates of Khariff Crops Due to the Flood and Cyclone of 1971
            in Orissa.* Bhubaneswar: Bureau of Statistics and Economics.

Grenell, Peter
    1972   "Planning for Invisible People: Some Consequences of Bureau-
            cratic Values and Practices." In *Freedom To Build* (ed. John
            F. C. Turner and Robert Fichter), pp. 95-121. New York:
            Macmillan.

Hunter, W.W.
    1872   *Orissa: Or the Vicissitudes of an Indian Province under Native
            and British Rule.* Reprinted in Sahu (ed.), Vol. 2.

Kolenda, Pauline
    1959   "A Multiple Scaling Technique for Caste Ranking." *Man in India* 39:115-26.

Kolenda, Pauline Mahar
    1963   "Toward a Model of the Hindu *Jajmani* System." *Human Organization* XXII (1):11-31. Reprinted in Dalton (ed.).

Levy, Marion J., Jr.
    1966   *Modernization and the Structure of Societies.* Princeton: Princeton University Press.

    1972   *Modernization: Latecomers and Survivors.* New York: Basic Books.

Lynch, Owen
    1969   *The Politics of Untouchability.* New York: Columbia University Press.

Mahar, Pauline. See Kolenda.
    1959

Mahar, Michael (ed.)
    1972   *The Untouchables in Contemporary India.* Tucson: University of Arizona Press.

Mandelbaum, David
    1964   "Introduction: Process and Structure in South Asian Religion." *Journal of Asian Studies* 23 (June):5-20

    1972   *Society in India.* Berkeley: University of California Press.

Marriott, McKim (ed.)
    1955   *Village India.* Chicago: University of Chicago Press.

    1960   *Caste Ranking and Community Structures in Five Regions of India and Pakistan.* Poona: Deccan College Postgraduate and Research Institute.

    1968   "Caste Ranking and Food Transactions: A Matrix Analysis." In *Structure and Change in Indian Society* (ed. Milton Singer and Bernard Cohn), pp. 133-71. Chicago: Aldine.

Miller, David M. and Dorothy C. Wertz
    1976   *Hindu Monastic Life: The Monks and Monasteries of Bhubaneswar.* Montreal and London: McGill-Queen's University Press.

Mishra, K.C.
    1971   *The Cult of Jagannatha.* Calcutta: K.M. Mukhopadhyay.

Misra, Sadasiva
    1961   *Economic Survey of Orissa,* Vol. 1. Cuttack: Government
            of Orissa, Finance Department.

Mitra, Rajendralala
    1880   *The Antiquities of Orissa,* Vol. 2. Calcutta: Wyman and
            Company. Reprint. Calcutta: Indian Studies Past and
            Present, 1963.

Mohanty, Gopinath
    1967   *Harijan* (in the Oriya language). Cuttack: Jagannath Rath.

Myrdal, Gunnar
    1968   *Asian Drama: An Inquiry into the Poverty of Nations.*
            New York: Pantheon.

O'Malley, L.
    1929   *Puri District Gazetteer.* Patna: Superintendent, Government
            Printing, Bihar and Orissa.

Panigrahi, K.C.
    1961   *Archaeological Remains at Bhubaneswar.* Bombay: Orient
            Longmans.

Panigrahi, C.
    1960   "Muktimandap Sabha of Brahmans, Puri." In *Data on Caste:
            Orissa* (ed. Nirmal Kumar Bose), pp. 189-92. Calcutta:
            Anthropological Survey of India.

Pattnaik, Nityananda and Ajit Kishore Ray
    1960   "Oilman or Teli." In *Data on Caste: Orissa* (ed. Nirmal
            Kumar Bose). Calcutta: Anthropological Survey of India.

Ramesan, N.
    1962   *Temples and Legends of Andhra Pradesh.* Bombay: Bharatiya
            Vidya Bhavan.

Randhawa, M.S.
    1974   *Green Revolution.* New York: John Wiley and Sons.

Rudolph, Lloyd and Susanne Rudolph
    1967   *The Modernity of Tradition.* Chicago: University of Chicago
            Press.

Sable, Alan
>   1976   *Paths Through the Labyrinth.* New Delhi: S. Chand and
>   Company.

Sahu, N.K. (ed.)
>   1956   *A History of Orissa.* Calcutta: Susil Gupta (India) Ltd.

Seymour, Susan
>   1975   "Some Determinants of Sex Roles in a Changing Indian Town."
>   *American Ethnologist* 4:757-69.

>   1976   "Child-rearing in India: A Case Study in Change and Modern-
>   ization." In *Socialization and Communication in Primary Groups*
>   (ed. Thomas Rhys Williams). *World Anthropology* Series of the
>   IX ICAES Congress. The Hague: Mouton.

>   in press "Caste/Class and Child-rearing in a Changing Indian Town."
>   *American Ethnologist.*

Shah, A.M.
>   1974   *The Household Dimension of the Family in India.* Berkeley:
>   University of California Press.

Silverberg, James (ed.)
>   1968   *Social Mobility in the Caste System in India.* The Hague:
>   Mouton.

Singer, Milton
>   1966   "The Modernization of Religious Beliefs." In *Modernization*
>   (ed. Myron Weiner), pp. 55-67. New York: Basic Books.

>   1972   *When a Great Tradition Modernizes.* New York: Praeger.

Singer, Milton and Bernard Cohn (eds.)
>   1968   *Structure and Change in Indian Society.* Chicago: Aldine.

Sinha, B.N.
>   1971   *Geography of Orissa.* New Delhi: National Book Trust, India.

Srinivas, M.N.
>   1966   *Social Change in Modern India.* Berkeley: University of
>   California Press.

Stein, Burton
>   1960   "The Economic Function of a Medieval South Indian Temple."
>   *Journal of Asian Studies* 19 (2):163-76.

Taub, Richard
    1969   *Bureaucrats under Stress.* Berkeley: University of California Press.

Vidyarthi, L.P.
    1961   *The Sacred Complex of Hindu Gaya.* Bombay: Asia Publishing House.

Wallace, Anthony
    1956   "Revitalization Movements." *American Anthropologist* 58:264-81.

    1966   *Religion: An Anthropological Approach.* New York: Random House.

    1970   *Culture and Personality.* 2d ed. New York: Random House.

Weber, Max
    1958   *The Religion of India.* Glencoe, Ill.: The Free Press.

Zimmer, Heinrich
    1946   *Myths and Symbols in Indian Art and Civilization.* New York: Bollingen Press.

Index*

*For Oriya language caste names, see page 31, Table 3.1.